Running Your Own
CATERING BUSINESS

Running Your Own

CATERING BUSINESS

Ursula Garner and Judy Ridgway

THE KOGAN PAGE
Working for Yourself
SERIES

First published in Great Britain in 1984
by Kogan Page Limited
120 Pentonville Road
London N1 9JN
Reprinted 1986

British Library Cataloguing in Publication Data
Garner, Ursula
 Running your own catering business.
 1. Food service management — Great Britain
 I. Title   II. Ridgway, Judy
 647'.95'068   TX911.3.M27

 ISBN 0-85038-842-2
 ISBN 0-85038-843-0 Pb

Printed and bound in Great Britain
by Anchor Brendon Ltd, Tiptree, Essex

Contents

Introduction

Small catering businesses have been sprouting like mushrooms in recent years and, despite the recession, many have prospered and some have grown into quite large outfits. Many who have come into the catering industry have been untrained either as professional chefs or as business men and women, but they have been good cooks, often with some first class specialities, and they have been keen to offer quality food backed up by friendly and efficient service. The formula certainly works at the small scale end of the catering market.

This type of firm generally works as a one-man band or as a partnership, backed up by teams of freelance kitchen and waiting staff. These are the small businesses referred to throughout the following text. Slightly larger or medium-sized catering companies may employ anything from two to a dozen or more full-time staff. Most of these will usually be in the kitchen or administration, with freelance back-up at the event. There are, of course, also some very large organisations who employ many more people and operate on a national or semi-national basis.

The progression from a small to a medium-sized business may come about as a natural result of increased business. However, it is far better to plan such expansion, particularly as it may mean a move to new premises and thus greater financial burdens, as well as an increase in the number of full-time staff. The latter also brings problems of supervision and maintenance of standards. The steps to even greater expansion need to be even more carefully thought out. Will the extra business come from increased volume in the same areas or will you need to diversify into new areas? Is the timing right both financially and in regard to the market place? Can your existing management cope with the extra volume of business? These are all questions which will need to be answered.

The scope of work carried out by catering companies is certainly wide enough to allow for more entries into the field but you will need to study your own area in some depth to see what kind of services might do well and whether or not they are already being offered by competitors.

Potential activities in the private sector take in every kind of function from christening parties to funeral teas and everything that happens in between! The list must include children's parties, birthday parties, engagement parties, weddings, anniversary parties, general drinks and buffet parties, retirement celebrations, luncheons, dinners, picnics, barbecues, brunch parties and late suppers and you can probably think of another dozen.

On the business front there are opportunities for catering for every type of meal from the desk-top lunch to a full banquet. There will also be buffets, brunches and maybe even breakfasts. Then there are group activities, such as club dinners and dances, large-scale barbecues and group travel hampers.

Some companies have built up their business by concentrating on one or two specialist services such as desk-top dining and picnics while others offer a comprehensive service. Some also combine their catering operations with related services such as dining suites, frozen food supplies or delicatessen shops.

Of course, thinking about running a catering company and actually doing so are two very different things and you will need to be very sure that you have what it takes. The first question is, how do you feel about hard work? You may reply that you are quite used to that but the truth of the matter is that hard work for an employer is nothing compared with hard work for yourself. You could be getting up at six in the morning to batch bake for the next day's wedding, spend the morning preparing a small buffet lunch and then supervising the service. This may be followed by a small cocktail party in the evening which drags on till nine or ten and then there are the records and accounts to fill in on those and yesterday's jobs.

In the early stages the chances are that you will also spend considerable time humping large bags and boxes of food, drink and equipment, from the cash and carry to your kitchen, from your kitchen to venues which will inevitably be on the second or third floor and thence back home again. So you must be physically strong and you will certainly need to have good health.

If you are not daunted by hard work then you should cast a look at your social life, for this could be the last you will see of it for some time. If you are involved in private catering you will find that, naturally, everyone wants to entertain in the evenings and at weekends. This will intensify on bank holidays and at Christmas and Easter. Even if you concentrate on dealing with business catering, you will still have the books to do in the evenings and batch cooking at the weekend, and the chances are that you will also be taking on the odd weekend wedding or large evening party simply because it can be lucrative.

The next question must be, how does your partner or family view the proposed venture? They will be the ones who will bear the brunt of the change in your social life and they could also be affected by the increase in kitchen use, your lack of time, and the need to steer clear of your office area.

Once you have faced these initial stumbling blocks, take a cool look at yourself and your personality. How are you at dealing with people? Your staff are essential to you and you must be able to get on with them, direct and support them. Your clients, too, must find you equally friendly, helpful and efficient.

Are you completely unflappable—even if the glasses have not turned up, the ice is melting before you can properly cool the champagne, and one of your helpers has just dropped a whole tray of canapés? How resourceful are you? Will you know how to roll out a batch of pastry in the absence of a rolling pin or open a beer bottle without an opener?

Having decided that you can cope with most eventualities, how much do you know about the catering business? If the answer is 'not very much' it might be worth working on a freelance basis for another outfit. This would certainly give you some experience in cooking and presenting the food, and if you keep your eyes open you should be able to learn quite a lot more.

There are also a number of courses which you might consider if you have the time and money to take a break between your current work and starting up your own business. These courses may cover the cooking (see Appendix) or they may cover the business side of your proposed activities. You will know which will be the most valuable to you.

When you have completed this kind of personal appraisal and perhaps undertaken some preliminary training, you will be in a much better position to take the decision on whether or not to go ahead with launching a new catering service. And once that decision is taken the groundwork can begin.

Chapters 1 to 11 look at the decisions that must be made before you can really get off the ground. Practical advice on the organisation of different kinds of functions follows in Chapters 12 to 18. Chapters 19 to 21 look at how to get your services known and how to build up a good reputation.

Chapter 1
Business Opportunities and Market Research

It is, of course, quite possible to set up as a caterer without any clear idea of what kind of business you are looking for and many small businesses have started off just like this. Such caterers have been prepared to turn their hands to anything, and slowly the business has trickled in and experience has gradually pointed the way to the more profitable business opportunities. But this is at best a rather haphazard method of going about things and at worst a recipe for low income, cash flow problems and possible bankruptcy.

Far better to assess all the possibilities in advance and to check out the most promising against some careful market research and your own inclinations. The latter consideration can be more important than sometimes given credit for. There is, after all, no point in setting up a dinner party service when you would really prefer to avoid evening work. Things could work out to start with, but you may find that as time goes on you lack the enthusiasm to keep the initial impetus going.

On the other hand, a dinner party service might fit in with your particular life-style very well indeed. But if your catchment area is largely inhabited by 30-year old couples with young children and fully stretched budgets you will have to think again. Equally, a popular retirement area will not be the place to start up a children's party service, and a small market town is unlikely to support a business based on desk-top lunches.

A detailed look at the potential market will help you to put together a much more viable business plan than would otherwise be the case. Such a plan, supported by detailed analysis, will be essential if you are thinking of trying to raise outside finance. It will also be an extremely useful guide when taking decisions on subjects as diverse as the type and amount of extra kitchen equipment to buy, putting together menus and prices, and planning a publicity campaign.

Catering activities

The best way to start a business plan is to list all the activities which a catering business might reasonably take on. Work with the checklist below. Expand sections as ideas occur to you and ignore any market information you have at this stage. It could inhibit your imagination, and the exercise is really a kind of brainstorming session which might throw up some unusual and possibly profitable ideas for the future. You can sort out the practical suggestions from the flights of fancy later on. All the activities mentioned are covered in greater detail in subsequent chapters.

Domestic market
The activities listed under this heading will all be intended for private individuals or groups of people organising their leisure pursuits.

1. Dinner parties
A dinner party service can work extremely well in a highly residential area with a reasonable level of wealth. Requirements will vary from those hostesses who require a complete service, including waiting on and washing up as well as shopping and preparation, to those who want only to have the food delivered so that they can pass it off as their own.

Numbers may vary from four to 40 but you will need to be aware of the pitfalls at both ends of that scale. Unless you have a specially adjusted price structure, four people can be quite uneconomic. On the other hand, 40 may present problems in the size and capacity of your cooking equipment and extra staff will probably be required.

Depending on the spending power of your potential customers, the business may be scattered among a large group of customers who will be using your services only for special occasions, or it may be confined to a much smaller group of regular clients. The latter business can spill over to orders to stock up for country weekends. There may also be some call for catered luncheons from such clients.

Jean Pierre Depesme of Jean Pierre's Pantry started with just such a group of regular and wealthy clients, and his frozen food business grew up in response to requests from customers for food similar to his dinner party offerings to take to their weekend residences. He gradually stocked up his first freezer by cooking between catering engagements to fill in time.

2. Buffet parties

This is another reasonably profitable area. A good many people will occasionally bring in outside caterers for their parties and if your catchment area is a good one, you could specialise in buffets. As with dinner parties, hostesses vary in their requirements and the demand may be for a complete service or simply for the delivery of the food. Numbers may vary from 12 or 20 to as many as 100 or more and you will certainly be involved with extra staff and catering equipment hire. The buffet may be finger or fork food.

3. Cocktail parties

These are unlikely to form the full basis for your activities but they can be extremely profitable. However, bear in mind that canapés can be extremely time-consuming to prepare and must be priced accordingly. Numbers may very from 20 to 200, and if you are providing a full service, extra staff will be required and special care will need to be taken with the drinks.

4. Weddings

Wedding breakfasts may take the form of a buffet or canapé party or they may be sit-down meals but, because of the special considerations involved, they do form a separate area of activity in their own right. As caterer, you will need to be an expert in wedding protocol, for you will often be called upon to advise the bride and her family. In the right area weddings

13

can be a lucrative speciality. Numbers may vary from 20-odd to 200 or more. In addition to the usual requirements, you may need to deal with marquee and furniture hire, provide the cake and act as master of ceremonies.

5. Anniversaries and special occasions
Like wedding breakfasts, these may take the form of a dinner, a buffet or a cocktail party, but by highlighting your expertise they can become an important profit centre. Janet Raglan's Catering Company is based in a wealthy retirement area and she has made a speciality of wedding anniversaries from pearl (30 years), through coral, ruby and sapphire to gold (50 years) and emerald and diamond.

The same idea might be exploited for younger age groups in other areas. Birthday parties, particularly for the decade, and retirement parties are other ideas. There may also be a call for catering specialised celebrations such as bar mitzvahs, coming of age parties or Hogmanay.

6. Children's parties
Children's tastes are quite different from those of adults and a successful party service could be inundated with business. Many mothers will say to a first time party-giver quite simply, 'Don't!' But if the preparation of the food and the organisation of the party are undertaken by the caterer, the mother has a much easier time. Numbers could vary from 12 to 20 — resist too large a number or it will be chaos. You may need to be able to organise games and entertainments as well as provide food, cake and presents. Theme parties are popular with children so make sure there are plenty of creative ideas in your brochure.

7. Outdoor parties and picnics
British weather being what it is, these are only likely to supplement your business during the summer months, but barbecues are growing in popularity and a specialised service in this area could catch on. All outdoor parties pose special problems but they can also offer something a little different.

Picnics and hampers can be a useful adjunct to your business, particularly if you are situated near famous beauty spots or the venues of well-known sporting events, such as race courses. One-off offers for annual events are also worth considering.

8. Specialised food catering
There are a small number of businesses which have made a success of specialising in wholefood or vegetarian menus. However, unless you are sure of your market, it is probably more sensible to offer such specialities as an additional service.

9. Catering for clubs and associations
Most residential areas abound with clubs and associations covering almost every type of leisure activity. Most of them have annual social events and many organise much more frequent get-togethers. A caterer specialising in just such events could be extremely welcome. The chances are that there could also be a useful spin-off into private functions.

10. Frozen food service
This is a fairly specialised activity which is sometimes run on its own and sometimes in conjunction with a general catering service. Opportunities include freezer stocking and the provision of complete frozen dinners and buffets. However, the larger operators offer a range of single portion dishes which can be purchased individually or in bulk.

The outlay for this type of operation is likely to be much higher than for a small catering business which could be started with minimum capital. Frozen food requires a considerable investment in freezers and bulk preparation and cooking equipment. New or extended premises will probably also be required both for the preparation and packing of the food and for the sales operation. Additional sales outlets will need to be ferreted out and a continuous supply of orders maintained.

11. Delicatessen caterers
This is another logical extension of the idea of catering

from special premises and quite a number of such shops have opened recently. The food is all prepared on the premises and sold both in the shop and through the catering business. The shop acts as a sampling operation as well as a retail outlet in its own right. Customers can choose the degree of service they require, coming to the shop or having the food delivered to their homes. Service and special menus will also be available.

12. Other catering activities
Once you have your own premises, the possibilities start to open out but, of course, so do the problems. Hiring out premises for social functions, for example, can work well in an area which has little in the way of function rooms other than the local hotels. Demonstration kitchen facilities could find a ready market in the major cities where PR activity is high. Training and cookery courses offer other possibilities.

Commercial market
These activities will all aim to provide a service for businesses in your catchment area. Some will be similar to those offered to the private market but there are differences in timing and organisation. Most business activity is likely to be at lunch time and on weekdays, whereas private functions tend to be in the evening and often at the weekend. Methods of payment will be another difference. Private clients will usually pay on the day or shortly after receiving your bill. Business customers are much more likely to sit on your invoice for a couple of months!

1. Business luncheons
This is likely to be by far the largest of all the commercial opportunities. Most business entertaining is done at lunch time and this holds good for small gatherings and large press receptions or VIP visits. Business meetings often carry on through the lunch period and the participants still need to eat.

   (a) *Sit-down luncheons*
      These are usually fairly small boardroom

affairs and you may need to work out a special price structure to ensure that they are profitable. However, larger numbers may be catered for at press functions and at Christmas time.

(b) *Buffet luncheons*

This is where the bulk of the business lies: conferences, press receptions, general receptions, annual, monthly and weekly meetings of trade federations and institutions, demonstrations, sales meetings and management/union meetings, openings and overseas visitors all provide the need for a meal. Buffets may be quite simple or extremely elaborate. Numbers are likely to vary from 20 to 200.

(c) *Cocktail and drinks parties*

These are more likely to be held in the evening but cocktails will be over by eight or nine o'clock. Small events may be held to mark presentations and retirements but larger events could run into hundreds. Evening drinks parties, possibly with a buffet, become much more frequent over the Christmas/New Year period.

(d) *Lunch and picnic boxes*

Lunch boxes or sandwiches and finger food may be ordered on a regular basis for office meetings and working lunches. They may also be ordered by senior executives who do not want to go out for a meal at lunch time but who have no in-house catering facilities. Picnic boxes may be ordered for public relations trips to sporting events and the like.

Your skills and inclinations

The second area to look at in some detail is your own skills and inclinations. Here are some questions to ask yourself. The answers will help you to cut down the list of possible activities discussed above.

1. Do you have any special training?
Answers may include a full-time catering course, cordon bleu training, some evening classes or nothing at all. If you are a good cook it will not matter if you have no training, but you must be sure that you will be able to cope with larger scale cooking and will be able to produce a particular dish which has been specially requested by your client. You must also be able to direct other cooks when catering for large functions or when your business expands. You may feel that you should add to your professional training and courses are listed in the Appendix.

2. Have you any special skills?
These may have been developed as a result of training courses or classes or they may just have been acquired over the years. Obviously, a skill in pastry- or bread-making, cake decorating or decoration work could point you towards a preference for particular activities. However, special skills are not essential. It is usually more useful to be a good all round cook. You can always buy in special expertise.

3. Have you any special inclinations?
What kind of things do you enjoy cooking? However good you are at a particular culinary activity, you will soon become bored if you do not enjoy doing it. A dinner party service, for example, will entail a quite different type of catering from that required for desktop lunches and picnic boxes.

4. What are your time constraints?
Are you prepared to work in the evenings and at weekends or would you prefer to restrict business, as far as possible, to lunch times and weekdays?

5. How large an operation are you planning initially?
The answer to this may depend on available capital or it may be tied up with your decision to take in partners or to employ people.

Market research

The next stage in putting your business plan together is to study your catchment area. The more detailed this study is the more useful it will be.

Start by defining your catchment area. This really means deciding how far you are prepared to travel to fill your order books. In a large city you may be able to draw a line round a five- or ten-mile radius. However, your study should also take in the surrounding area, for you may find that the addition of a further five miles in one direction will bring you into a much wealthier area or will enable you to consider business luncheons.

Most caterers running businesses based outside the large conurbations accept that, from time to time, they will probably have to travel quite considerable distances.

Next, try to assess your catchment area in terms of life-style, tastes and spending power. Here are some of the factors on which you should check:

Local population trends
Is the population expanding or decreasing? What is the average age of that population? Figures for the past five years should show the trends. Check your local council for figures or ask your local library to help you to track them down. This information will help you decide if the area is predominantly a retirement area, a haven for the wealthy middle-aged or simply full of young couples with children.

Income trends and wealth
What is the average income in the area and thus what kind of spending power? Assess this by driving round the area to look at the property: talk to estate agents and to local rate assessment officers.

Group activities, clubs and leisure complexes
A look at the kind of local activities that are available will help to reinforce your conclusions on life-style and spending power. It may also point to specific markets. Check if there are any sporting venues such

as race courses or sports stadia. Is there a permanent show or exhibition site?

Business and industry
What is happening to business in the area? Is it expanding or contracting? This could be important both for private and business functions. New industrial estates will mean a larger number of executives moving into the area. They may also mean a greater potential for business entertaining. Are there any really large firms, government departments or large insurance companies in the area? All these may generate business. Talk to local planning officers, check the Yellow Pages and the phone book.

Competition
It is also important to look at the potential competition. Their activities may be useful in assessing the market. There may be gaps in their repertoires which you could usefully fill. Check the Yellow Pages and any other local directories and walk round the area to look at delicatessen and specialist shops.

Checklist of potential business
From the above research you should be able to make a list of different categories of potential customers, together with an indication of the kind of services each group might be interested in. Here are a couple of hypothetical examples.

The first covers a large seaside town with a large retirement population but also with a wealthy residential area to one end and a thriving tourist trade. Leisure activities include a busy sailing club, a well-known operatic venue and a large sports complex. There is also a small industrial estate and the head office of a major distribution company.

Private functions
Retired population. One-off anniversaries and family gatherings.
Wealthy inhabitants. Dinner party service and larger parties. Hampers and picnics.

Sailing, tennis, cricket and bowling clubs. Club functions.

Operatic venues. Hamper service for the season.

Tourist track. Special hamper service through hotels which do not have a large enough staff to fulfil demand.

Industrial estates and headquarters of distribution company. Business lunches, desk top and buffet, for meetings and for entertaining. One-off functions at Christmas.

The second example covers a residential area about seven miles from the centre of one of Britain's largest cities. The local population is fairly young but with a reasonable income.

Business community. All kinds of business functions including desk-top lunches, buffets and cocktail parties and PR events.

Local population. Children's parties. Buffet parties and barbecues. Club functions.

The opportunities here are very much greater than in the first example and the decision to concentrate on business or private functions will probably depend more on your own inclinations than on the potential volume of work. Once that decision is made you should go back and look at the relevant markets in more detail. In the seaside town, on the other hand, it may be necessary to explore all avenues of potential business before you are in a position to decide which to concentrate upon.

By working with the above three checklists you should now be in a position to write out a fairly realistic assessment of the pattern of potential business for your firm.

Chapter 2
Finance

It is possible to start up a small catering company with very little initial capital. Your own kitchen may be suitable for use and you can hire any special equipment. Extra staff can be used on a spasmodic and freelance basis and changes can be made as you gradually plough profits back into the business. All you really need is the small amount of working capital to finance your first two or three months' trading. Remember that this will need to include sufficient to pay yourself a living wage.

However, if you are really serious about the business you will probably need to make a greater investment than this. The sums involved will depend upon the size of business operation you have in mind and upon the type of catering activities on which you expect to major. The business plan outlined in the previous chapter should provide the guidelines here.

Estimating the finance required

To estimate the amount of money you will need, check through the following areas of expenditure:

Premises
Will your existing kitchen be suitable or are you planning to set up the business in quite separate premises? If a shop forms part of the business plan or if you are thinking of setting up demonstration kitchens or catering facilities for hire, then this will form the major part of the fixed capital requirement.

If you are planning to use your existing kitchen in your private residence, it may need to be extended or redesigned and refurbished to satisfy the requirements of the Food Hygiene Regulations (see pages 32-3) and this too could cost quite a lot of money.

Capital equipment

After the structural considerations, there is equipment to consider. New premises will, of course, demand new or perhaps second-hand equipment but it all needs to be purchased before you can start up.

Your own kitchen may need the addition of large cookers and greater storage space. You may have to buy new mixing and processing equipment, larger pans and special utensils or bakeware. Serving dishes will need to be considered and you may decide to stock up with sufficient plate, glasses and cutlery to be able to provide for small functions without hiring. See Chapter 6 for more details of possible requirements.

Capital equipment may also take in office equipment such as typewriters, answerphone, desk and duplicating equipment.

Transport

It is almost impossible to run a catering business without some form of transport. This is the time to decide whether or not you need a new car, estate car or van, or whether you can manage with the one you have.

Starting-up costs

There are costs which will be incurred simply by starting up. These could include stationery and office materials, menus and price-lists, packaging materials and bulk purchase of groceries. Ask yourself what you will need for your own particular operation. If, for example, you are planning to specialise in hampers and picnics, you will require a supply of the actual hampers and picnic boxes to hand. A desk-top dining service will call for a good stock of paper plates, plastic crockery and paper napkins, and a speciality line in cakes and desserts will require cake boxes.

Starting-up costs might also include new telephone installation charges, insurance on the business and its transport, legal fees and publicity.

Working capital
Last but by no means least you will need the money to buy the food and pay the other bills incurred during your first few months of trading. To determine how much this is likely to be, you will need to work out an estimated budget and cash flow forecasts. These will support any business proposal you put together to back up requests for capital to banks and other financial institutions. In addition, they will be very useful tools in assessing whether or not your pricing system is right, and in seeing how your business is faring (see page 29).

Organising the business

As soon as you have estimated the costs involved in setting up, you will need to start talking to your bank manager, solicitor and accountant. But before you do this, you must also have some idea of what sort of business you are planning. What is its legal entity to be? You may be planning to go it alone or you may feel that the business plan you have in mind needs more than one person to manage and control it. You may even have prospective partners or directors in mind.

However, there are some very relevant advantages and disadvantages attached to the formation of partnerships and private limited companies, and you would be well advised to talk to your accountant and solicitor, or read the relevant section of *Working for Yourself: the Daily Telegraph Guide to Self-employment*. Indeed, your accountant and solicitor and above all, your bank manager, are going to be extremely important to you both in the initial organisation and setting up of your business and in the running of it. If you already have good working relationships with such people it is sensible to stick with them. If you haven't, the choices will be important ones.

Start by talking to other business people in the area and see who they are using. If you are already in touch with one local adviser or you know your bank manager well, ask him to make some recommendations.

Get together a short list of suitable firms in each field and take your time about the choice. Do not simply go to the nearest. Go and see each firm on your list. Make a list of items to check and questions to ask. Be clear in your own mind about the areas in which you think you will need help.

Raising the money

The more money you can raise yourself the easier it will be to get going, so start by working out just how much you can put together from your own resources.

Possible sources of personal finance

1. Have you any spare capital in building societies and the like?
2. Have you any shares or securities which could be sold or used as security against a personal loan?
3. Have you just received redundancy pay or a retirement annuity?
4. Have you any jewellery, paintings or antiques which might be sold?
5. Have you a second home, a caravan or a boat which might also be sold?
6. Do you have any insurance policies against which a loan might be negotiated?
7. Is there a chance of a second mortgage on your house or could you sell up and buy a smaller, cheaper one? The latter might be the easier course if you are married and need your partner's agreement to a second mortgage.
8. Your business partners, if you have decided upon a partnership, may also be able to raise money in the same ways.

Depending on your circumstances and on how ambitious your business plan is, these methods may produce sufficient money to go ahead. If they do not then they may still provide enough to enable you to get a loan for the rest.

Bank loans
The bank is the most likely source for the money you

25

need and may be prepared to offer a lump sum towards any initial investment required. It may also offer an overdraft facility to help with the demands upon working capital. This is the commonest form of bank help and it has the advantage that interest is paid only on the actual amount you are overdrawn. The disadvantage is that an overdraft can be withdrawn at any time, so it should be used only to cover short-term requirements.

The bank may ask for personal guarantees for the money they are prepared to lend you. Larger branches are more likely to lend larger sums than the smaller branches but if you can get a small branch to invest in you there are advantages in the closer relationship you are likely to establish there.

Some banks run their own start-up schemes and some foreign banks are reputed to be freer with the risk capital. So shop around but keep your solicitor and accountant fully informed of your intentions and be sure they check the small print in any agreement.

Information on government loan schemes is available from any Small Firms Centre, a division of the Department of Employment. Telephone freefone Enterprise for your nearest office.

Private loans
Very often the difference between the total of your own capital and that required to start up in business can be found within the family or from friends or ex-business associates who are prepared to back your ideas. The best way to arrange this is for your backers to guarantee a loan or overdraft on the basis that, if the recipient is unable to pay up, then the guarantor is liable for that amount. The advantages of this kind of arrangement are that, in certain circumstances, the guarantor of a business loan can treat any losses incurred as capital losses which can be used to offset capital gains. Details are given in a pamphlet available from any Small Firms Centre.

The outright loan of capital sums can be fraught with difficulty, however. First, it must be made clear to what extent, if any, the lender has any say in the running of the business and what the nature of this control is. Such control is to be avoided if possible and the existence of a loan should not normally entitle the lender to any participation in management matters nor to a share of the profits.

Misunderstandings can also occur concerning the terms of the loan, and the best plan is to get a solicitor to draw them up formally, covering the rate of interest, the duration of the loan and how it is to be repaid, the circumstances under which the loan may be withdrawn and any other conditions.

Sometimes private loans, and indeed those from other outside agencies such as finance houses and investment companies, are conditional on acquiring shares or the option to acquire them. You should try to avoid this for it means that you will be giving away part of the company and you are unlikely ever to get it back.

Other sources of finance
If you are planning a major operation with new premises you may need to look further afield for the larger amount of capital involved. Possible sources include regional development boards, the Council for Small Industries in Rural Areas, merchant banks and finance houses such as the Industrial and Commercial Finance Corporation. *Working for Yourself: the Daily Telegraph Guide to Self-employment* contains a very useful section on finance.

If, on the other hand, you need only a small amount to help you keep going the 1983 Budget introduced the Enterprise Allowance Scheme whereby, if you have been unemployed, you can receive a grant from the DHSS of £40 a week for 52 weeks. You need to have a viable idea for starting your own business and be prepared to put £1000 of your own money into it.

It is well worth considering hire purchase agreements if most of your requirement is for a car or van or for equipment such as cookers or freezers. This is a useful way of financing medium-term commitments. The payment is spread over a period of time and, until the period of the agreement expires, the item remains the property of the finance company and the borrower does not have to provide security as is the case with a loan. However, rates of interest can be high and it is worth getting more than one quote if you can.

Putting together a business proposal

This does not have to be as complicated as it sounds, but it can be invaluable in showing that you have studied your market prospects in detail and understand how the proposed business should be run. The bank manager or investment company will be looking for an assessment of the business potential, of the services you plan to offer, detailed breakdown of starting-up costs and budget, cash flow and profit forecasts. What your proposals should show is that you understand the business you plan to enter and have a clear idea of how things will go. A typical proposal will include the following headings:

Personal and company details
Details of the proposed structure of your firm together with the names and addresses of the partners and directors, if any. It should include an outline of your own history and that of anyone else involved, with details of relevant experience and qualifications.

The business plan
This will be taken from the business plan worked out in Chapter 1. It will outline the type of work on which you expect to concentrate, together with any specialised sidelines which could add to the overall profitability of the business. This information should be supplied by the market research information you have gleaned.

Financial requirements
Details of all the money needed for the purchase of premises or capital equipment as well as that required under the headings of starting-up costs and working capital. It should be itemised in some detail and a further section may be required to give full details of new premises, planning permission, surveyor reports etc. This should be followed by a breakdown of the

money already available from personal or other sources and that which is still required.

Sample menus and price-lists

These will include a detailed breakdown of how the prices are computed and an estimate of the volume of business required to break even.

Budget for the first six months of operation

The budget will include a month-by-month or week-by-week estimate of income and expenditure, the latter being broken down into fixed and variable costs. If business is expected to be seasonal, the budget may need to be projected for a year or longer. Notes on how the estimated income has been arrived at should also be included.

Cash flow forecast

This will cover the same income and expenditure information contained in the budget, but instead of being averaged out over the entire period, the sums will be shown as actual amounts in the months in which they fall. Starting-up costs may be included in the first month (see page 23).

References

This section will give names and addresses of financial referees.

The preparation of this business plan will clarify your ideas, and enable you to discuss all aspects of the project both fluently and objectively with potential lenders.

It is worth writing up such a business proposal even if you do not really need any outside finance. It will certainly provide a very good base from which to start. When you have written it, have another look at the financial requirements, and ask yourself, 'Have I covered every eventuality?' It may be sensible to add in a little more to cover something which may cost more than you have budgeted or which you simply have not thought of.

Next ask the complementary question: 'Do I really

need to spend all this money at this stage?' This question is even more important if you are going to borrow the money to cover that spend. It is not wise to over-commit yourself. Far better to start off in a smaller way and build up the business over time than to suddenly find you cannot make ends meet.

Chapter 3
The Legal Requirements

Once you set up in business there is a mass of legislation which needs to be taken into account. It covers subjects as diverse as the hygiene of your kitchen, the details printed on your packaging, the way you treat your employees and the records you will need to keep. Some of the legislation could affect you even before you start trading. You will, for example, need to have planning permission from your local authority, and the Environmental Health Officer will probably want to inspect your kitchen.

Most of the relevant Acts of Parliament are pretty complicated and you may need to take expert advice in various areas. However, some government and local government departments issue booklets explaining what the requirements are and how they are likely to affect particular businesses. Copies of the Acts themselves can be obtained from HMSO headquarters and HMSO bookshops and a study of these, together with any explanatory booklets which are available, should point you in the right direction.

The various areas affected by legislation are:

The premises

In theory, you need to have planning permission for any kind of change in the use of a building, and if you are planning to run your business from home this could be seen as involving a change of use for at least part of the time. In practice such a change may not be evident from the outside and will probably not result in any inconvenience to the neighbours or any change to the nature of the area. However, the local council could order you to stop trading from your house if they found out about your activities and objected to them.

The need for planning permission becomes much more acute if you buy or rent property outside your home. If the property has previously been used for other purposes you must get planning permission from the local authority for a change of use. This holds good even if the premises have been used as a shop or restaurant before. However, the nearer the previous use to your current proposals, the more forthcoming permission is likely to be.

Whatever the previous use, it is only sensible to plan your application in some detail and to research it well. The Planning Committee will want to know exactly what you are planning to do, how these plans will affect the immediate neighbourhood and what demand there may be for your particular services. Make sure that you include structural plans and detailed drawings with your application and do list absolutely everything that you hope to do to the building.

Extensions to your existing property must also be submitted for planning permission and you would do well to check with your local Fire Officer and Environmental Health Officer before submitting your plans. There may be some requirements you have not taken into account. The Occupiers Liability Act, for example, covers the duty of the occupier of premises to visitors to those premises, and the Health and Safety at Work Act makes provision for good lighting, ventilation, toilet facilities and the like for employees.

The Food Hygiene (General) Regulations is probably the most important piece of legislation in this area. It comes under the umbrella of the Food and Drugs Act, Section 16 of which requires you to register with your local authority the moment you make food for sale. This means contacting your local Department of Environmental Health. These regulations take in all aspects of the cleanliness of your premises and cover the structural make-up as well as the kitchen surfaces, ventilation, washing facilities, equipment, drainage, storage and refuse. Some councils issue useful guidelines or notes on their requirements and the inspectors are usually extremely helpful when it comes to planning new premises or making changes to existing ones.

Checklist of relevant legislation
Fire Precautions Act 1946
Food and Drugs Act 1955
Food Hygiene (General) Regulations 1970
Health and Safety at Work Act 1974
Occupiers Liability Act 1957
Offices, Shops and Railway Premises Act 1963
Shops Act 1950

The food

Once you have got your premises sorted out and start to plan your menus, or the food to offer for sale from the freezer or over the counter, you will come up against the next batch of legislation.

Some foods such as sausages, meat pies etc have very strict standards for their composition, and if you are planning to sell them you will need to check with the regulations. However, most of these refer to the meat content levels which are so low that any quality product is likely to be way over the specifications. The use of preservatives in food is also regulated and this may also affect your operation.

If you are planning to include a frozen food service in your activities then the Food Labelling Regulations will come into force. This legislation requires quite a lot of information to be included on the label. You must, for example, state the name and address of the maker, a list of ingredients in descending order of weight, the precise name of the food, an indication of shelf life and how it should be stored, and any special instructions for use. All this information must be easy to read and easy to understand.

Claims made for your produce must be within the limits of the Trade Descriptions Acts, and you will also need to have a working knowledge of the Weights and Measures Act.

Checklist of relevant legislation
The Meat Pie and Sausage Roll Regulations 1967*

Meat Products and Spreadable Fish Products
  Regulations 1984
The Miscellaneous Additive to Food Regulations
  1980
The Food Labelling Regulations 1980
Trade Descriptions Acts 1968 and 1972
Weights and Measures Acts 1963 and 1976

Running the business

The Sale of Goods Act and legislation dealing with
the hygiene of delivery vans will affect you when the
planning stages are over and you start to trade.

You will also become liable for income tax and,
possibly, corporation tax. Value added tax will also
have to be paid. Unlike income tax, it is calculated on
the turnover of your business rather than on the
money you make after paying all the costs. The VAT
limit is currently set at £19,500 (1985 figure) per
annum or £6500 in the last calendar quarter and,
unless your business is very small indeed, you will be
liable from the start. You register for VAT at the
local Customs and Excise office and you should find
the VAT inspectors very helpful indeed. If you are in
any doubt about how to carry out your obligations
they will usually arrange to visit you.

If you are employing people, even if only on a part-
time basis, you will also be liable for organising their
income tax deduction under the PAYE scheme and
for National Insurance contributions both for yourself and your staff. Employing staff will also involve
you in the mass of employment legislation covering
everything from conditions of dismissal and redundancy, through accidents and disease reporting, to
race and sex discrimination. The Inland Revenue and
the DHSS both publish numerous leaflets for
employers.

The way round some of this legislation is to employ
only casual labour on a one-off job basis. The individuals so employed will be responsible for dealing with
their own tax and National Insurance but you are
still liable for the standards of work under the

hygiene regulations and for the provision of suitable conditions of work.

Checklist of relevant legislation
Articles and Substances in Contact with Food
    Regulations
Employers Liability Act 1969
Employment Protection (Consolidation) Act 1978
Employment Acts 1980 and 1982
Equal Pay Act 1970
Fair Wages Resolution 1946
Food Hygiene (Market Stalls and Delivery
    Vehicles) Regulations 1966
Information for Employees Regulations 1965
Race Relations Act 1976
Sale of Goods Act 1979
Sex Discrimination Act 1975
Social Securities Acts 1978 and 1979
Unfair Contract Terms Act 1977

Insurance

This is an extremely important subject that often gets overlooked. First of all, some form of insurance may be a legal necessity. If, for example, you employ staff on the premises, even if only part time, you are legally bound to take out approved policies from authorised insurers against liability for injury or disease sustained by your employees in the course of their work.

Your customers, too, need to be protected and you should most certainly take out some form of public liability insurance in case you cause food poisoning or some other kind of injury to your customers. You will also need to cover yourself in case your waitresses break anything in a client's home, the freezer breaks down or you have a fire in the kitchen. You will also need to insure your premises and your means of transport.

Checklist for insurance
Employers' liability

Public liability and third party public liability
Premises insurance and consequential loss of
    business
Cover for all contents of the premises and
    consequential loss of business
Vehicle insurance
Insurance against loss of driving licence
Legal insurance against prosecution under the
    relevant legislation affecting your business
Insurance of stock and consequential loss of
    business

If you are operating from home or using an existing privately owned car, you should check with the various insurance companies that the change of use will not affect the existing policies.

Insurance is expensive and, though it is essential in that it is far better to be safe than sorry, you do want to be sure that you are spending your money in the best possible way. Start off by going to a reputable broker. He will help you to find your way through the mass of different policies, but make the final decision yourself. Whittle the choices down to two or three and then read the policies in detail and with careful attention to the small print. Consult your accountant and solicitor; they may be able to indicate advantages or pitfalls you had not noticed. Once the decisions have been taken and you have policies on the go, you must remember to pay the premiums on the due dates and to update values periodically so that the contents insurance and the like represent current replacement values.

Chapter 4
Choosing Your Company Name

It is worth giving a good deal of thought to the choice of a name for your business, for once you are operating, you will be stuck with it. It takes enough time to build up a reputation without losing it and having to start again just because you no longer like the name under which you are trading.

Points to consider

The name you choose can set the whole tone for your operation. Here are some points to bear in mind when choosing a name.

Is it memorable? By and large, short names are easier to remember than long ones but, if a longer name is particularly apt, it may well stick in the mind even more.

Is it easy to pronounce? If so, it will be easy to communicate to others and word-of-mouth recommendation is extremely valuable to a catering company. Words which are difficult to pronounce do not get spoken so often for many people will avoid using a word if they are not sure of its pronunciation.

Does it clearly establish the nature of the services you are offering? Clever names are all very well but, if their message is not immediately clear, their businesses may be overlooked. Prospective customers leafing through the Yellow Pages or reading your advertising must be able to match your activities to their needs.

Does the name create the right sort of image for your business? There is no point in going for the wrong sort of slang expression if you are looking for upper-crust business. Equally, a very grand name will tend

37

to discourage customers looking for something fairly cheap and cheerful! Your name should inspire confidence among your potential clientele and should convey the impression that you are a professional outfit and know what you are doing.

Does anyone else trade under a similar name? Obviously, you cannot trade under the same name as someone else—particularly if they are already operating as a limited company. This would infringe the legal protection of that company's name. Even if the other company had no protection for their name, you would hardly want to attract business for them, which could happen if you set up a particularly successful service. Check the Yellow Pages in your own and surrounding areas before going ahead. If you are setting up a limited company the name would then have to be checked with the Registrar of Companies before you could complete the formalities.

Does the name lend itself to the design of a logo? Some companies, particularly those with long names, operate with a shortened version of the name or with the initials. This kind of abbreviation can lead to the use of a monogram or logo made up of the initials. In other instances, a drawing is used in conjunction with the company name to make a letterheading, which can help to make the business name more memorable. Maple Leaf Catering, for example, might use a drawing, realistic or stylised, of an actual maple leaf, whereas Jackson and Rhodes Ltd might use the combined letters J and R.

Will the name be acceptable to the Registrar of Companies should you wish to set up a limited company? The use of words which could mislead the public by suggesting that an enterprise is larger or more prestigious than it really is is a case in point.

Names fall largely into four categories. Examples, both real and imaginary, are given below for each category. Have a look through them and see which type you think would be most appropriate for you.

The proprietor's name

Both christian names and surnames feature among

the many catering businesses in the telephone directory. Some are very formal, such as Ring and Brymer, Blakes and Rothsey Clarke. Others are chattier with names such as Claire's Kitchen, Chez Paulette or Jane and John. Some of these stand as they are but most of them are qualified by the words Caterers, Catering, Party Service or Picnics. This is only sensible, for otherwise potential customers will have no idea that your services meet their needs.

The location

Some catering companies such as London Cooks, City Caterers, Country Cooks and Aylesbury Catering have taken their names from their locations. This can be a good idea provided that the name does not seem to imply that the caterer will not or cannot operate outside the area designated.

The food

By far the most popular names are those which have a connection with eating or with entertaining. Gluttons, Plum Duff, Food To Your Door, Fresh-Bite, Party-Fare, Carvers, High Table, Party Planners, Above the Salt, and Travelling Gourmet are just a few of them.

General themes

Other names have been chosen with reference to all kinds of ideas, symbols and sayings, which presumably just happened to appeal to their owners: By Word of Mouth, Black Cat Caterers, Maple Leaf Caterers, Other People's Houses and Contessa. There may be no link between this kind of name and the services offered and so it is only sensible to add a word such as 'Caterers' or 'Cooks'.

Once chosen, the name will be used on all stationery including letterheadings, invoices, cards, compliment slips, menus and price-lists and also on your premises, delivery boxes, labels and perhaps your van or car.

Remember that if the name you have chosen is different from your own, then the Companies Act requires you to show the latter on all stationery and at your place of business, and this applies whether or not you are organised as a limited company.

Your name and the stationery on which it appears will be an important ambassador for your business and it is worth paying a good designer to suggest possible logos, together with layout and lettering. Choose just one design and use it on everything. You will achieve much more impact from constant repetition than you would by using a different layout or lettering on each item. You may also decide to choose a house colour at this stage but do not just follow your own personal preferences. Choosing red because you like it may not be as sound as choosing royal blue because it projects a solid professional image. Your designer should also be helpful here.

Remember that the end result is supposed to help you to project an image of your business. Go back and look at your business plan. What sort of image do you think will appeal most to your potential customers? Try to define the kind of image you want to put across and then explain this to the designer, who needs to be thoroughly briefed if he or she is to produce a design that really works for you.

Chapter 5
Location and Premises

For some businesses location is vital. For a catering business location is important but it will not have the same impact as it might on a restaurant or a wine bar. This is just as well, for many catering businesses are set up from the proprietor's own home. If you are starting off from home, the location is fixed and you can only re-check your market research and plan to specialise in those areas around you which seem to offer the most profit. The advantage that an outside catering business has over a bar or restaurant is that it is mobile and can take its services into those areas that have more potential custom.

Location

Of course, if you have decided to buy or rent premises specially for the business or you are planning to run a home-made delicatessen shop in conjunction with your catering service, location can become more critical. Nearness to potential customers will be particularly important to a shop, but an area with low rents may be more important for premises which will only be concerned with preparation, cooking and storage.

Being near potential customers may involve proximity to the business section of the town or being in a wealthy residential area. Whatever your speciality, the majority of your business will come from word-of-mouth recommendation. If you are planning a shop, then nearness to potential customers will also mean good passing trade, and it may be that the High Street will be a far better location for it than a small block of suburban shops.

The only way to check on passing trade in any location is quite literally to stand and count it. Do this at

41

potentially quiet times as well as during peak shopping hours. Have a look, too, at the other shops in the immediate area. You can learn quite a lot about the location and indeed about the inhabitants of the town itself from the shops in the High Street. The presence of McDonald's, for example, usually means plenty of passing trade, and a Marks & Spencer shows a certain spending power. Check the quality of the shops in the neighbourhood and their merchandise. Do the greengrocers sell out-of-season fruit and vegetables along with the cheaper ones, what sort of specialist lines do the grocers carry, are there any high fashion names on show in the boutiques or dress shops? The answers to such questions will point to the sort of area it is.

Buying or renting premises

The decision on whether to buy or rent depends not only upon locational considerations but also on the requirements of the business, the amount of money you may be able to raise, and what is available. Unfortunately, the last factor often exerts more influence than the others. Time is usually short and, unless you are already operating from home and simply want to expand, or you have a permanent job to keep you going until you have found an approximation to the ideal premises, the pressures will be on to find somewhere as quickly as possible.

Check back to your business plan and then write out a specification for yourself which you can refer to as you inspect properties. Here are some of the points which might need to be considered when checking a prospective property.

Nearness to potential customers. See the remarks on location above.

Previous use. Has the building been used for similar purposes? If not, you will almost certainly have to get planning permission. You will also need to check the facilities with more care to see that there are no problems with essential services. The fact that there is a tap or drainage pipe in place does not mean that it is attached to anything!

Approximate size and layout. Will the layout affect

the way in which you can use the premises? Do you need or want to be all on one floor or on different floors? A catering operation with function rooms, for example, may be much more convenient to run if it is all on one floor, whereas a shop and catering business could operate quite well with the kitchens on one floor and the shop on another.

Structural changes. How much will have to be done to the building to make it suitable for your use and will it take the structural changes involved? And, of course, the next question is, can you afford to do all that needs doing? Check the layout of water pipes and mains services against your plans for they could affect the arrangement of your kitchen.

Approximate cost range, including the desirability of freehold, leasehold or rental. If you have decided on rented accommodation you will need to look at the lease carefully to see that there are no prohibitions of use and that there is an acceptable renewal clause.

When you have found a property which seems to match up to your specifications, or at least approximates to them, you should bring in your professional advisers. Your solicitor will check the lease and any other legal factors and your accountant can advise on the price level and costings. To this battery of advice you should also add a surveyor. His report could help you to avoid numerous pitfalls.

Once you have the benefit of all this professional advice, stop and look again at the premises in the light of your business plan and specification. Take a long hard look. Is it really the property for you? Do not settle for the first premises you see, however good they appear. Inspect half a dozen or so to get a feel for what is available. Finally, give some thought to why the previous tenants are moving out. Do not just accept the reasons which are given to you. Dig a little deeper. There may be facts unknown to you and which may affect your decision to buy.

Refitting

Whether you are looking at the refurbishing of your

own kitchen at home or you are starting from scratch in new premises, the first step is to familiarise yourself with the requirements of the Food Hygiene (General) Regulations 1970 (see also page 32). You must ensure, for example, that the whole area is easy to clean and that there are no nooks and crannies which might house vermin.

You may need to install window or ceiling air extractors and ventilators, you may need another sink unit—the regulations state that unprepared food should be washed in a different sink from that used for washing up—and wash basins for yourself and your staff. Storage of food between cooking and cooling is important, and longer term storage will also need to be looked at. Here is a checklist of some of the factors:

Kitchen checklist:
Ceiling. Easily cleanable.
Walls and woodwork. Easily cleanable with no panelling or hidden interstices at the back of fitted equipment which could collect dust or house vermin.
Floor. Easily cleanable and made of impervious durable material. You must almost literally be able to 'eat off the floor' and you must keep it that way.
Ventilation. Window extractor/ventilator and canopy over the cookers. Check siting of fridge and freezer equipment which can give off heat.
Lighting. The lighting should reach a minimum of 20 lumens per square foot at working level. Consider whether an extra window would be preferable to a higher level of electric lighting.
Electrics. Are there sufficient sockets for all the equipment you expect to install? Have any danger points been checked out for possible overloading.
Work space. There must be sufficient space for everyone likely to be working in the kitchen and for any particularly extensive requirements such as filling picnic or luncheon boxes. The surfaces should be impervious and washable.
Washing and drainage facilities. Double sink units and separate toilet facilities for staff. If appliances such as refuse disposal units or potato peelers are to

be plumbed in, are the pipes large enough to clear properly?

Equipment. This should all be movable for cleaning and easily cleanable in itself. (See Chapter 6.)

Storage. Adequate ventilation in the larder and sufficient fridge and freezer space. The storage of refuse is also very important. Do you have adequate space and containers both inside the kitchen for short-term storage and outside for longer term storage? (See Chapter 9.)

If you are planning to set up a freezer service you may need a speedier method of chilling food than simply leaving it to cool. Food which has been prepared and is waiting to be packed or delivered must not only be properly covered, it must also not be kept between the temperatures of 500°F/100°C and 145°F/62.7°C. Serious outbreaks of food poisoning have occurred because caterers have left food in lukewarm conditions.

This is also the time to think about kitchen planning. The siting of all your equipment in relation to each other and to your work surface can be very important. Think, too, about the work flow within the kitchen area. In what sequence are you most likely to be using equipment and how many people will probably be working in each area at any one time? Draw up a sample plan and then mark on it the possible activity schedules. This will show if you have any potential bottlenecks or if a particular piece of equipment is to be in an inefficient location.

If you are planning to do a major operation with a delicatessen shop, or catering premises for hire, then you will also need to think in some detail about the fitting out of these areas. Here's an outline checklist of points to consider:

Checklist for refitting the rest of your premises
Customer capacity. How much of the total area is or should be designated for customer use? How many people are you aiming to seat in function rooms or how many people would you hope to let browse in the shop?

Work flow. It is important to determine the flow of food from the kitchen to the function rooms or to the shop. The flow of staff going about their business and the flow of customers into and around your premises also need to be considered. Passage to and from storage areas should not be forgotten here.

Display. This is obviously a vital factor in the design of a shop and should take in the window area, shelf and wall display and the counter.

Atmosphere. After the practicalities have been considered the next stage is to think about the effect you want to achieve. Once this has been decided it will help you to choose colour schemes and accessories.

The exterior. The exterior of your premises can also be an advertisement for your business, so you do not want to run out of money before you get around to considering the outside. Remember, too, that you may have to make provision outside for delivery trucks and possibly even customer parking.

Chapter 6
Equipment

The range of equipment available is so enormous that it is impossible to discuss the subject in detail in one chapter. Innovations in techniques and design are appearing all the time, and any analysis tends to become out of date in no time at all.

The small caterer who starts off working from home will naturally use the cookers and gadgets at his disposal, gradually buying larger, heavier duty items as business expands. Others may rent business premises and need to equip their kitchens from scratch. In both cases the golden rule is to research thoroughly before buying. Equipping a kitchen is a major outlay whether this is done over a period of time or in one fell swoop, and as a caterer you must be as cost conscious over this as over every other aspect of the business.

Criteria for buying

Quality and durability are vitally important. The equipment will be in constant heavy use and, though it may seem more expensive at first glance, equipment that is tailored to the catering trade is built to stand up to these strains and will be cheaper in the long run. Domestic equipment (particularly processors and mixers) is not built for heavy duty work and will need replacing after a surprisingly short period.

Hygiene is another point to consider when purchasing equipment. Strict rules are laid down for hygiene in commercial kitchens (see pages 32-3). Make sure that any items you consider buying have the scratch-free, easy cleaning surfaces that the health regulations demand.

Think, too, about how easy it will be to keep clean.

How easily does each piece dismantle, how easy will it be to reach the interior surfaces to clean them, do the cookers have a self-cleaning programme, how easily and quickly will the fridges and freezers defrost? You want equipment that takes the minimum amount of time and effort to keep clean, apart from enabling you to keep the highest standards of hygiene. Equipment that is easy to clean will keep your overheads down.

Safety in the kitchen is as important as hygiene, so bear this in mind each time you look at a piece of equipment. Do the doors open in a way which increases the likelihood of the staff burning themselves? Are the lids of the water heaters hinged or loose—steam can cause terrible scalds? What safety devices are there on the deep fat fryer? Does the meat slicer have a guard? Are the handles of pans sufficiently robust? Are the pans portable or will they be too heavy to move when full? Are the oven heights right or will there be accidents lifting heavy pots in and out?

If you have any doubts about the safety of an item, raise it with the manufacturer or check with your local Health and Safety Officer. Also make sure that your safety precautions include a first aid kit and fire extinguishers. The Health and Safety Officer will insist on these and again will advise on the most suitable types for your needs. He will also advise on where they will best be placed in the kitchen.

The efficiency of each item is a point to look out for too. You will want to know the capacity of each item, how long it takes to heat up or cool down, what the power consumption is. These details can vary enormously from one product to another and it is only by researching and comparing the different performances that you will be able to identify which is the most efficient and cost effective for your needs.

But how do you find out about the products which are available? Trade papers such as *Caterer & Hotelkeeper* are excellent sources of information as the editorial pages feature reviews of new products in both equipment and food, and they are crammed with advertisements for heavy and light duty equipment.

There is also an annual exhibition held in London each January called Hotelympia. This is well worth a visit as all the major manufacturers attend and you will have a chance to see their products in action. There are also a number of small exhibitions held in the provinces throughout the year.

Keep a look out for local sales of caterers' equipment. Here you can pick up stock from manufacturers that have gone bankrupt or equipment from caterers that have closed down. They are usually run on the same basis as auction sales with a preview day so that the public can browse through the lots in comfort and decide what to bid for.

And finally, do remember to enquire about discounts if you are buying large stocks of equipment or spending a lot of money with the supplier. Just as with food and drink, equipment suppliers will have discounts for bulk purchases or large orders. There might also be a case for buying on HP or even for hiring, so talk to your accountant.

Heavy equipment

Ovens
Used for roasting, braising and baking, ovens should have a good even temperature distribution. A poorly insulated oven will lose heat and increase your fuel bills, so check this too. Test the shelves, fittings and burners to see how easily they can be cleaned. Does the oven have a self-cleaning programme? Think about which way you want the oven doors to open and check that the height is suitable for lifting heavy weights in and out.

Grills
These can either be incorporated in the oven unit or they can come as separate pieces of equipment altogether. The sort that have doors double as ovens and can be a boon if you suddenly need extra oven space.

Frying
Both shallow fryers and deep fat fryers create a lot of grease and need to be convenient to clean. Ideally, the

kitchen should have three fryers, one each for fish, meat and vegetables. The small or freelance caterer is unlikely to be able to afford the money or the space for this number and will manage by changing the cooking oil frequently. Everyone knows about the fire risks attached to frying. Look for equipment which has the very best and most up-to-date safety controls.

Boiling, stewing and steaming

This is equipment which cooks food in moist conditions, not dry. One problem with these cooking methods is the volume and weight of the water. One gallon of water weighs 10 lb so it will just not be possible to move large full pans around the kitchen. For large-scale catering, the units should be fixed and have taps for filling and draining off. If the units are free standing, check that the height will be convenient and safe for stirring. Steaming can be done in a double boiler, a pressure cooker or a steam oven. If you are looking at pressure cookers, remember to check the safety controls as pressure cooking, like frying, can be hazardous.

Hot cupboards

These units are absolutely invaluable for keeping food and dishes at the right temperature over a period of time. Sometimes food has to travel a long distance from the kitchen to the dining-room. Other times, because of the quantity of food being prepared, some dishes will have to be cooked well in advance and kept warm. In both instances, the hot cupboard does the job admirably. A bain marie is another excellent piece of equipment for keeping food at the right temperature without spoiling. Both come in fixed unit and mobile trolley models.

Water boilers

These come in a wide range of sizes but when full, even the smallest will be difficult to move. With fixed units, look out for efficient in/out taps. All units should have a gauge glass which indicates how full the boiler is. They should be thermostatically controlled too, otherwise your water and fuel bills will simply boil away uncontrolled. To compare the performance of different models, check the capacities, the length of time taken to reach boiling point and the fuel consumption. Some boilers have an automatic refill system which tops up in small doses so that the water never goes off the boil for more than a few moments. Others are instantaneous heaters; the advantage here is that the water doesn't stand boiling for long periods and go flat. Be careful to check the output of this type of heater as some may be too low to be practicable.

Water heaters
The catering kitchen uses a tremendous amount of hot water each day for washing up, cleaning and cooking. Make sure the system is really efficient and is not going to let you down by running cold at regular intervals. Check the capacity, output and costs of various models before choosing.

Refrigerators
Ideally meat, fish and other food should be stored in separate fridges but, for small firms, this is just not practicable. Careful storage can prevent pungent food affecting others, but never store raw meat alongside cooked meat for fear of bacteria spreading.

In a busy kitchen the fridge door will be opened several times an hour. Each time it is opened the temperature rises and in no time at all it will be absolutely perfect for breeding bacteria. Some catering fridges have an instant cooling system which comes into operation every time the door is opened and keeps the interior temperature at the desired level. Large companies will have walk-in fridges and cold rooms. Apart from checking the efficiency of different makes, check that the doors open from the inside as well as the outside. And with all refrigerating units, check the defrosting and cleaning systems as well as the capacity and fuel consumption.

Freezers
The choice between chest and upright freezers will

probably depend on the amount of space you have available and on the volume of your business. Upright freezers take up less floor space and are thus more easily housed where space is at a premium, but chest freezers can be packed more efficiently and will hold more. They hold large packs of food better than upright freezers as there are no shelves to contend with.

For either type of freezer you will need to keep notes on the contents: what dishes it contains, where these will be found and when they went in. Whether your turnover is large or small, the contents must be consumed in date order, otherwise the food in the most inaccessible parts will never be used and eventually have to be thrown away.

Others

Sinks—ideally with waste disposal units, but certainly with the hygienic surfaces required by the health regulations, and lots of draining space. *Dishwashers* to cope with all the kitchen washing up and also all the crockery, cutlery and glassware that comes back dirty from each function. If you are not going to use a laundry service, invest in a good, large *washing machine*, a *tumble drier*, a *steam iron* and *ironing board*. The amount of laundry generated by catering is quite staggering—table-cloths, napkins, drying-up cloths, aprons, overalls, towels and oven gloves—all need regular laundering. It is also worth investing in a good *scrubbing and polishing machine* for the kitchen floor.

Glasses, crockery and cutlery

Buying these items can be an expensive exercise, so to start with you may decide to hire as and when you need them. When a pattern of your crockery and cutlery requirements begins to emerge, you will be able to assess whether it is worth investing in your own stocks. The next question you will be faced with is how much crockery and cutlery to buy. If the bulk of your work is small functions for up to 60 people with the occasional large reception for 150 to 200 people, you obviously won't want to tie your capital up by buying 18 or 20 dozen of everything. Better to buy six dozen sets and then hire in for the large functions.

When you do buy, make sure that you choose a standard line that can be replaced or added to. Choose designs that are plain as fussy patterns and loud colours will detract from the look of the food and may not be to your clients' liking. Also be sure to choose crockery that is durable, as it is, hopefully, going to be in constant use. Crockery and cutlery are costly items to stock up on, so it may be tempting to try to save money and buy cheaper lines. This is entirely false economy, however, as you will find it chips and breaks far too easily and you will forever be buying replacements.

Transport

To start with, you may be able to get away with using an ordinary car and hire vans for the larger functions. When your business has grown and a regular pattern of large orders is established you will want to think about buying your own van. Whether you go for the small, bread vans or larger traditional vans will depend on your work profile. If your work is mainly catering for smaller functions, you will go for the small vans. If you specialise in mass catering you will need the large ones. Shop around before buying either as you may well get some discounts and do check the cost of purchasing and running the vehicles against the cost of hiring. You want to be sure that you will make savings, and it will not necessarily be cheaper to buy and maintain your own transport when you bear in mind the cost of insurance, tax, depreciation, maintenance and fuel.

Chapter 7
Setting up the Business Systems

Accounts and records are a vital part of any business and it is important to get them right from the start. Accounts are, of course, a legal requirement for any business which is registered for VAT, and also for limited companies. You will have to satisfy the demands of the Inland Revenue too, and this is much easier if you have proper accounts.

If you are not sure just what sort of accounting systems to use, read the rest of this section and then talk to your accountant. He will be able to advise on the best methods to suit your particular type of business but, unless you are prepared to spend a fortune, do not expect him to do them for you. Some companies are large enough to justify the services of a part- or full-time book-keeper. If yours is not, you will have to keep the books yourself.

All too often business failures are due to inadequate record keeping. The owner feels that time spent running the business is more important than writing up the ledgers. This attitude is very short sighted for it means that a mass of paperwork will accumulate which could take weeks to sort out, whereas time spent after each job writing up the accounts and records need not be too onerous.

In addition to the time saved, the accounts and records will be much more accurate and you will be able to see trends in the business much more quickly. The kind of records to keep will vary depending on the type of business you are running, but they could include individual job or customer records which will show how accurate your estimating is, which dishes or menus are the most popular and when to start changing the food on offer. Stock control records could be important if you are offering your own label wine or have a system of bulk buying for groceries, accessories or accompaniments. You will also need to keep a note of the whereabouts of equipment, cutlery, crockery and glasses, and a staff book is useful if you are using a lot of casual labour.

Accounting records

The essential books are cash books. They make up a complete record of all the money coming into the business and all the money going out. The records covering money going out will probably need to be broken down into three books: the cheque payments book, the cash payments book, and petty cash. The reason for the extra cash payments book is that in a catering operation quite large sums are likely to be paid out in cash both for food and staff and these items are not really petty cash items.

Cheque payments book
This will record all the money going out of your bank account. Think very carefully about all the expenses you are likely to incur and buy the widest cash analysis book you can find. Arrange those categories across the top with three columns at one end for VAT, the total amount spent less VAT and the total plus VAT. List outgoings in date order and total every month or every three months to coincide with your VAT returns. These records will show you how much VAT to claim back, where all your money is going, and whether there are any areas which need looking at in more detail.

The category headings should include those in the sample entry shown, plus Clerical, Telephone, Gas, Electricity, Depreciation, Rates contribution, Accountancy, Miscellaneous, and perhaps others too. The sample is based on a business run from home. If you have separate premises, additional entries will be required for rent and rates, maintenance and replacement of display equipment.

It is a good idea to work out a numbering system which relates to invoices, vouchers, receipts and cheque stubs. Do not just rely on the cheque number,

Cheque Payments Book

Receipt no	Cheque no	Date paid	Details	Total £	Total less VAT £	VAT £
1	216740	1.5.84	Butcher	64.00	—	—
2	1	1.5.84	Wine merchant	400.00	340.00	60.00
—	2	2.5.84	Cash	300.00	—	—
3	3	2.5.84	J Smith (Cook)	114.00	—	—
4	4	4.5.84	Mutual Life	300.00	—	—
5	5	7.5.84	Florist	16.00	13.60	2.40
6	6	7.5.84	John Lewis	190.00	161.14	28.86
7	7	8.5.84	Catering Hire Ltd	36.00	30.60	5.40
8	8	10.5.84	Cash 'n Carry	140.00	—	—
9	9	11.5.84	Petty cash	50.00	—	—

Cheque Payments Book

Job no	Food £	Drink £	Staff		Hire charge £	Flowers £	Equipment £	Insurance £
			Cook £	Waiting £				
1	64.00							
—		400.00						
1								
2	55.00		45.00	10.00				
—								300.00
—						16.00		
—							190.00	
1					36.00			
—	140.00							
—								

but number each transaction in the book and repeat that number on the relevant paperwork. Where possible it is also useful to relate the entry to the particular job. Use the job numbers from your customer records book (see pages 63-4).

Cash payments book

This will be similar in some ways to the cheque payments book but the headings are not likely to be anything like so extensive. The totals here will account for money entered in the cheque payments book to cash. Remember to include a column for cash in.

Petty cash book

This is a record of all the small cash payments made for postage, petrol, small items of stationery and the like. You will need to keep a cash float for such immediate purchases. Keep bills wherever possible and remember to include columns for cash in and for VAT. If your business is not very large this book could be combined with the cash payment book.

Receipt book

This is the income side of the cash books and will record all the money, whether in cash or cheques, that is paid into your business. It can serve as a useful guide to where the majority of your income comes from, so break down the sections to give you as much information as possible. The VAT due on each transaction must also be recorded along with a bank column in which are listed payments into the bank from your paying-in book.

The sample shown on pages 60-61 is based on a small catering company operating from home.

Invoice records

A home sales day book can be useful in keeping track of money owed to you. If you keep all your invoices in date order and you are mainly dealing with private clients who pay on the spot, you may not need to keep a home sales day book. If, on the other hand, your customers are likely to take their time in paying your bills, this kind of record will serve as a reminder to chivy them up a bit.

Use prenumbered invoices or, if you have your own printed invoice forms, remember to have the appropriate number typed in each time an invoice is prepared. Keep a copy of every invoice in a loose leaf file as a double check.

Enter every invoice in the home sales day book as you send it out or present it to a client. List invoices in number and date order and make room for information on the recipient, the total amount due, the VAT amount, and any special terms such as discounts for early payment and dates due. Finally, remember to include a date paid column. As long as the column remains empty it will remind you to send out statements and, if necessary, ring for payment.

Total the home sales day book monthly and do not leave any invoices outstanding without some sort of reminder. Do make sure that the initial invoice goes out promptly. You are more likely to be paid quickly at the time of the service than if you leave it for weeks before sending out your invoice.

Purchase records

For some businesses these records will be unnecessary, but if you are buying a lot of supplies on credit it may be useful to have a purchase day book. This records all the purchases made on credit together with details of the date, the supplier, the invoice total, VAT amount and the date of eventual settlement. It may also include reference to a purchase order or requisition and to discounts or penalties for prompt or slow payment.

It can be useful for a business to defer payment as long as possible and these records ensure that you do not defer them for too long or forget to pay altogether, both of which will inevitably get you a bad reputation. You will probably find that some suppliers press for payment fairly quickly whereas others are much slower. It is not dishonest to take advantage of the difference and pay the former first.

Receipt Book

Date	Total £	VAT £	Total less VAT £	Job no	Business functions				
					Food £	Wine £	Buffet £	Formal £	Cocktail £
8.5.84	494.00	74.10	419.90	4	494.00	494.00			
10.5.84	86.00	12.90	73.10	2	86.00		86.00		
11.5.84	865.00	129.75	735.25	3					
16.5.84	116.20	17.43	98.77	6	116.20	116.20			
16.5.84	76.50	11.47	65.03	5	76.50		76.50		
17.5.84	97.00	14.55	82.45	7					
19.5.84	427.50	64.12	363.40	1	427.50	427.50			
21.5.84	650.50	97.57	552.93	8					

Cash Payments Book

Paid in £	Date	Receipt no	Details	Job no	Total £	Total less VAT £
300.00	2.5.84		From bank account			
	3.5.84		To shopping	1	116.00	
	3.5.84		To staff	1	77.00	
	4.5.84		To staff	2	49.00	
	4.5.84		To shopping	2	48.10	

Receipt book

Private functions						Bank £
Food £	Wine £	Buffet £	Formal £	Cocktail £	Weddings £	
296.40	568.60				865.00	1445.00
						192.70
97.00				97.00		97.00
386.50	264.00	650.50				

Cash Payments Book

VAT £	Food £	Drink £	Cooks £	Waiting Staff £	Clerical £	Flowers £
	35.00	66.00				15.00
			35.00	42.00		
			35.00	14.00		
	18,00	26.00				

Wages and capital records

If you employ staff on anything other than a casual basis you will need to keep a wages book. This shows the gross earnings for each employee together with deductions for tax, National Insurance, pension contributions, net pay and the employer's National Insurance contributions. You will also be responsible for deducting PAYE at source.

If you have made a large investment in capital equipment for your kitchen or you have fixtures and fittings in outside premises, you may need to keep a capital ledger. The method of accounting for these items is different from that for day-to-day purchases and should be discussed with your accountant.

From the records described above your accountant will be able to get together the information needed to compile a trading and profit and loss account and a balance sheet. However, it will only be necessary to produce these if you are trading as a limited company.

Cash control and profitability

It is vital for any business to have sufficient money coming in to meet the demands of paying for goods and services, and in this instance, paying for food and casual staff. It is sometimes possible, particularly with private clients, to ask for 50 per cent of the estimated cost in advance of the event you will be catering. This will certainly cover most of the purchases which have to be made in advance and some of the staffing costs. As well as acting as a cash flow cushion, it also covers you for cancellations. However, not all your customers will agree to this kind of arrangement and you will need to keep a careful eye on your cash flow situation. Failure to look ahead can lead to an expensive overdraft or an irate bank manager and sometimes both!

You should really work out a budget forecast and a cash flow forecast before starting up in business and they will be an essential part of any proposal to gain added finance. Once you are operating, these forecasts can be revised in the light of actual performance.

Your budget should show the estimated monthly incomings, and against these are set the outgoings. This will necessitate some shrewd guesswork if you have not run this type of business before, so beware of over-optimism. Fixed costs are averaged out over the period of the forecast. At the base of the page are the net profit or loss figures and the sum total of these will give you an idea of the overall profit levels to expect. You may need to work out forecasts for periods of six months, a year and three years. Talk to your accountant for the most useful periods to look at.

The cash flow forecast, on the other hand, shows the same series of figures, but instead of averaging out the fixed costs over the period concerned they are entered at the time they are actually due. The profit and loss figures at the base now show if there are sufficient funds to cover a very large invoice. You may have a reasonably profitable company but could find yourself short of ready cash if a large bill is due to be paid and you have a large wedding and some other big jobs to finance. It is very difficult to predict ahead in the catering business and so the estimated figures at the top of the forecast should be updated as soon as any particularly large group of events seem to be coming up all together. It will most certainly affect your short-term cash flow forecast. It's a good idea here to keep a wall diary or bookings chart so you can see such a situation arising. The chart will also help to prevent you taking on more than you can handle at any one time.

Customer and job records

The records outlined so far will tell you how profitable your business is; they will also tell you where the money is coming from and where it is going to. What they can only indicate but cannot detail is whether your estimating and pricing are accurate. To do this you will need to keep detailed customer and job records.

These records should show your estimate of costs and the quotation given to the client, together with any relevant calculations. After the event the actual costs can be filled in. Make a note of major discrepancies together with an indication of the possible reasons for them. These records will be invaluable for your future pricing policy.

Such records will also be extremely useful in pinpointing popular dishes or menus and in keeping a note of bad payers or difficult personnel. A typical customer record sheet may be set out as follows:

Customer Record Sheet

Name of customer
Contact:
Secondary contacts if necessary:
Address and tel no
Notes on the venue, kitchen facilities, etc
Notes on preferences, idiosyncracies etc
Payment record

Job no	*Date*	*Details*	*Menu Estimates*
			Actual costs
Job no	*Date*	*Details*	*Menu Estimates*
			Actual costs

Staff record book

If you are using a lot of casual labour, it is extremely useful to have a record of who is reliable, how far they are prepared to travel, what their particular skills are and how they work with other people.

A small notebook is all that is required. Keep a page or half page for each person you work with and classify the booklet by job function, such as cooks, waitresses, waiters, barmen, butlers, washing-up staff and so on. Obviously, you will need to include their names, addresses and telephone numbers together with notes on the factors listed above. It might be useful to star the best people so that you can find them quickly.

Equipment hire

Some catering businesses have large stocks of their own crockery and the like which can be used by clients. Even if you do not go this far you may often find that you are leaving serving dishes at a client's house. You may also leave some stuff behind by mistake. It is very easy to lose track of your equipment in these circumstances.

To be sure of always finding missing equipment, keep a book in which every loan is entered. You could even extend this to your own use, so if a particular dish is to be used at a particular event, the job number of that event is entered against that piece of equipment in the book. You will then always be able to see where the item was last used. Such a record might be pasted on the storage cupboard door or on the shelving.

Stock control

If your business is fairly small you may not be doing very much bulk buying, but a larger business may have quite large stocks of certain items in store. It will also be employing staff who may not be quite as honest as they seem. Security is a major problem for most businesses and it is unlikely that yours will be the exception. Other catering companies invest in their own label wine and this is another expensive item which needs to be accounted for.

Stock records need not be very complicated: a record of the date the stock went into store, its quantity, and when each item is removed and for what purpose will suffice. The time you really need to watch stock is during transfer and when it is at the venue. Bottles of wine and other items from a full bar have a habit of 'walking' if you do not have a tight system of personal control.

Office procedures

It is important to designate an area in your home or premises as an office, where you can work undisturbed. Here you can keep all your records, stationery stocks and office equipment such as typewriter, filing cabinets and home computer if you decide to go to this level of sophistication.

It is fairly easy to buy all your accounts and record books, but make sure you have worked out exactly what you will need in advance, otherwise you may find that there are insufficient columns or the design just does not suit your plan.

There are also a number of pre-planned office systems from companies like Kalamazoo and Twinlock and as some of these have been designed with small businesses in mind, you might find they suit you better. Many are self-duplicating so that, with one line of writing, you have made entries in several sets of records or maybe written a cheque as well. But beware, the salesman can be very persuasive and you could find that you have bought a system which is not ideal for your particular operation. So shop around, talk to your accountant, and plan in detail before committing yourself.

Chapter 8

Brochure and Menu Design

There is no doubt that a carefully researched and well-planned menu and price-list will win you business, whereas a hastily prepared, ill-conceived one will be dropped straight in the waste-paper basket. Most people looking for a caterer will ask a number of firms to send in their brochures. Competition is likely to be strong, and unless the brochure has been pitched at the right level, it will be disregarded immediately. All the time and money spent on planning and printing will have been utterly wasted.

Planning

When planning menus and price-lists, return to your business plan (see Chapter 1). In practice, it is unlikely that a firm would restrict itself to one market segment entirely—it will usually choose its main market and then pitch its image to appeal to the segments immediately either side as well. You may have chosen to specialise in catering for a middle market of people who want good quality food at sensible prices, but are also prepared to cater for large low budget functions using mass produced food and also for small up-market gourmet functions. Alternatively, you may have decided to concentrate on delivering high class working lunches to businesses but will also cater for directors' lunches and cocktail parties. The brochure should reflect this flexibility in the copy and in the range of menus and prices featured.

Having identified your market, the next step is to research the service offered by your competitors. What is the quality and style of their brochures, do they include photographs and illustrations, are many different examples of menus given, what prices are they are charging, does the price per head include waitress service and hire charges, are ancillary services offered, is VAT included in the price, are discounts given for large numbers or prompt payment?

Obviously, the range of services and prices will differ from firm to firm but it should be possible to identify those that will be your direct competitors. Once you have armed yourself with all this information, you will be able to prepare a brochure that will compete favourably against rival firms. Clearly, your brochure won't win you every job you quote for. What it will do is maximise your chances of winning orders by creating the right image.

The brochure

Brochures should always be sent out with a covering letter. This makes the client feel that he is getting personal attention, and also enables you to fine tune the details of your services even more closely to each enquiry. For instance, you may realise that, although the client has asked for details of a three course sit-down meal, his budget will only stretch to a two course fork buffet. A covering letter can tactfully point the client in this direction, highlighting the various advantages to be gained by a change of plan.

The brochure is very important as it creates an image of your company and its services in the client's mind. Large firms may employ a commercial artist to do the design, in which case, it will be worth while preparing a written design brief. This will not only clarify your thoughts but will also give the designer a clear understanding of the image required and prevent him wasting time and money producing unsuitable layouts. Small firms may not be able to justify the expense of employing a professional designer; however, most printing firms will help out here with examples of other brochures they have produced and guidance on type-faces, weight of print etc.

Ideally, you should try to use a designer and printer who have been personally recommended. If you have no contacts in this field, approach three or four of each and choose the one that seems to offer the right quality of work at a sensible price. Any design work will probably be charged at a flat fee, but the print fee will depend on the number of brochures to be printed. The longer the print run, the cheaper the unit cost. Be careful not to be influenced by this into overestimating the number of brochures you need. It's no good reducing the unit cost but then having thousands of brochures sitting idle in your storeroom.

If there are to be no photographs or illustrations, the brochure can be livened up by choosing coloured paper or coloured inks for the printing. Design features like this need careful consideration though, as they can have expensive implications. Will coloured paper mean you have to buy coloured envelopes as well? These can be quite costly. Will the firm's notepaper have to be coloured too to complete the image? General stationery costs could rise dramatically.

The menu

There are two main schools of thought here: some firms (mainly the large ones) compile a range of set menus and work to these almost exclusively; others put together a few sample menus, purely to illustrate the style of their work, but make a point of planning menus individually for each function. The former system is less time-consuming, cutting out repetitive menu planning, and is particularly suitable for the mass market — sit-down meals for two or three hundred, fork buffets for large wedding receptions, cocktail snacks for gala nights. Once the menus have been drawn up, only the prices need updating.

Tailor-made menus obviously take up a lot more time but this can be costed into the prices charged. At the more exclusive end of the market, there is a definite call for this sort of personal service. Also, if you have a number of regular customers you will need to plan menus individually as you can't keep offering the same dishes week after week.

Menu planning will not present much of a problem if you restrict yourself to set menus or plain food. However, if you are offering an individual service or specialising in imaginative food, you may often find yourself running out of inspiration. Build up a good library of cookery books and refer to these regularly to prevent your ideas from going stale. This can be an expensive exercise, but by investing in two or three classic volumes and borrowing others from your local library, costs can be kept well down.

The classic cookery books will be an excellent source for traditional dishes but books on specialist food—eastern cookery, Elizabethan cookery, vegetarian cookery etc—will be very useful too. Some of the dishes may have to be adapted but by familiarising yourself with as wide a variety of cooking styles and techniques as possible you will build up a considerable repertoire that can be continually extended. Many clients will not be familiar with the names given to classic or foreign dishes and particularly sauces. What *is* chicken chasseur? What *is* a bearnaise sauce exactly? Bear this point in mind when compiling your brochure; it might be worth giving brief, mouth-watering descriptions of each dish.

The secret of successful menu planning is not only a matter of selecting appetising dishes that are appropriate to the occasion, but also keeping the courses balanced. For instance, a rich and creamy main course should be preceded by a light starter and followed by a refreshing dessert. Make sure the vegetables complement the main course. If this is plain, serve vegetables with sauces. If the main course is rich, serve vegetables that are plainly cooked. Roast and fried vegetables are delicious but may be too rich for the rest of the menu. Don't serve seafood as a starter if the main course is fish.

For cocktail snacks and finger buffets, aim at a balanced mixture of pastry and bread based items, fish, meat, dairy products, vegetables and fruit. Bear in mind the colours and textures of the food. Adding a touch of red or yellow will bring a plate to life. Spiced apricots will brighten up a dish of cold chicken—and taste delicious too. Coarse pâté should not be followed by a chunky casserole—far better to precede this with a smooth mousse or a crunchy vegetable dish. Avoid soup as a starter if the main course is in a sauce and the dessert in syrup.

The list is endless but paying attention to this sort of detail will enable you to plan balanced menus that will delight your guests, not send them away groaning with indigestion.

Chapter 9

Quantities, Purchasing and Storage

Quantities

If you are just starting up in catering, probably your biggest nightmare will be the question of getting quantities right. There is always the dread that there won't be enough food to go round and that guests will be jostling for the few last morsels. Even when it is obvious that enough food has been provided, the temptation to add just a little bit more to be on the safe side can be overpowering. Don't give in to this. On the safe side you might be, but your profits certainly won't. Every ounce of extra food is costing you money and reducing your profits. Also, your client will not appreciate seeing trays of untouched food which are the result of over-estimating portions. He will conclude that, had he employed a caterer who knew what he was doing, the price per head would have been considerably lower. This may not be true but it is the natural conclusion for him to draw.

There are practical problems associated with over-estimating quantities too. If you provide too much food you will be faced with the problem of having to dispose of all the leftovers at the end of the reception. A lot of function rooms insist that the caterer takes the rubbish away with him and you could find yourself repacking and carting large quantities of wasted food away with you.

So how do you cope with the problem? It won't take long to develop a sixth sense about quantities but this is hardly a professional attitude. Every caterer must have a set of basic guidelines from which to work and this becomes more important when estimating for large functions, as any wastage will be multiplied. Similarly, it will be important when your company grows and you have to hand down tasks like estimating quantities to your staff. The only way to be sure of making accurate assessments is to work from a list of tried and tested formulas.

Obviously, no formula can be applied across the board. There will be cases where allowances have to be made and you should always ask yourself, once you have worked out the initial estimate, whether there are any circumstances which will involve increasing or decreasing the quantities.

- Will there be children among the guests who will eat only half portions?
- Will the guests have come from playing sport, in which case their appetites will probably be larger than normal?
- Will they be going on to dinner and perhaps resist eating too many of your cocktail snacks so as not to spoil their appetites?
- Is the menu too rich for large portions?
- Is the function being held in the open air when people often eat more?

These and other considerations could lead you to adjust the size of your portions either up or down.

However carefully you work out your estimates, sooner or later you will be faced with the problem of unexpected guests turning up and needing to be fed. It is, therefore, a good idea to allow for one or two extra people in all your estimates and to cost these into your price per head. When the number of unexpected guests is more than simply one or two, all you can do is instruct the waitresses to reduce the portion sizes. If your waitresses are good they will be able to cope with this portion control discreetly though, obviously, if there are scores of extra mouths to feed there will be a point when there just is not enough to go round.

The well-known rule that, as numbers of guests go up, the quantities of food come down, is only partly true and can be misleading. This rule really only applies to small gatherings where there will be more wastage in preparation and cooking than for large functions. Guests at a gathering of 1000 will have just as large appetites as guests at a gathering of 300 and therefore need the same size portions. It is true that there will be savings when you are catering for large numbers but these savings will not be in the quantities of food you provide but in the cost of that food. By buying in greater bulk, you will get discounts and special prices which will reduce the unit cost of each dish.

Estimating quantities for a mixed buffet will require a slightly different approach from the norm. Whereas the individual portion for a single main dish of, say, chicken may be 4 to 6 oz, the quantities allowed for a mixed buffet of chicken, seaford tart and ham mousse will differ. The chicken portion will be reduced to 2 oz per head and the tart and mousse calculated at one third each of the normal portion size. There is another point to bear in mind when estimating quantities for mixed buffets. Will one of the dishes be more popular than the others? This is usually the case and rather than disappoint people by running out of the favourite early on, you should try to provide a greater proportion of those dishes that you know are particularly popular.

Converting recipes
What about recipes—how can these be adapted to large quantities? The secret here is to convert all measures to weights and then multiply these up to suit the number of people you are catering for. Three level tablespoons of flour equal 1 ounce. An egg white is equivalent to 1 fluid ounce. So to convert a recipe for four people calling for, among other ingredients, 3 tablespoons of flour and two egg whites, to quantities for 40 people, the ingredients become 10 oz flour and 20 fluid oz egg whites.

When cooking in quantity, you will also need to think about the size and shape of the dishes you are using and work out how these will affect the cooking times. They will increase, but not necessarily on a pro rata basis. For instance, food in a wide, shallow pan will cook more quickly than food in a deep one. Joints of meat are affected in the same way—a long joint with a small diameter will cook more quickly than a shorter-joint with a wide diameter. Get to know how long your large pans and ovens take to heat up so that you can switch them on in advance and not waste time waiting for them to reach the right temperature. It is surprising how long large utensils take to heat.

Surprisingly enough, your staff can affect the quantities of food you get through. If they are wasteful and careless, you will need to provide more food. Make sure they are all conscientious about wasting as little as possible. Train them to peel and prepare vegetables with the minimum wastage, to scrape out bowls thoroughly, to cut accurate portions, to handle food without damaging it. These tips may sound petty and hardly worth the effort but they will increase efficiency and reduce wastage. Remember that, although the wastage from one meal may seem insignificant, if you multiply this over a year, it will be quite substantial.

If you apply all the basic principles described here you will soon find that the task of estimating quantities is not nearly as difficult as you had first imagined. The table of quantities given will, hopefully, make this task even easier.

Purchasing

Although purchasing and storage are two different areas of activity, they are closely related and it is therefore sensible to look at them together. A shortage of space will restrict purchasing power. On the other hand, the storage facilities may be dictated by the firm's purchasing policy. It may be decided that larger premises with more storage should be found so that the company undertake greater bulk purchasing.

There are also other areas of overlap: cash flow, shelf life, seasonal buys, proximity of suppliers, transport costs, stock control, storage techniques and so on. Each must be weighed up so that well-planned and systematic purchasing and storage policies can be developed that will make the most effective and economic use of a firm's resources. For the freelance cook this will simply mean considering how

Item	Per head	Per 100 portions
Meat		
On the bone	4-6 oz	25 lb
Boneless	3-4 oz	20 lb
Stews and pies	2-3 oz	16 lb
Fish		
With lots of bone	6-8 oz	35 lb
Little or no bone	4 oz	25 lb
Vegetables		
Fresh green	4-6 oz	28 lb
Fresh spinach	8 oz	50 lb
Potatoes	4-6 oz	22 lb
Root vegetables	4-6 oz	22 lb
Pulses and rice	2 oz	12 lb
Sweets		
Pastry	1½ oz flour	10 lb
Sponge or suet pudding	1½ oz flour	10 lb
Milk puddings	3 to 1 pt	16 qt
Batter pancakes	5-6 to 1 pt	10 qt
Yorkshire pudding	6-8 to 1 pt	8 qt
Custard	6-8 to 1 pt	8 qt
Fruit for stewing	6-8 oz	40-50 lb
Fruit for pie	4-6 oz	25-35 lb
Dried fruit	1½-2 oz	10-12 lb
Miscellaneous		
Soup	2-3 portions to 1 pt	16 qt
Gravy	8 portions to 1 pt	6 qt
Coffee	3 (breakfast) cups to 1 pt black	
	6 (after dinner) cups to 1 pt black	
Milk		16 qt for white coffee allowing 2 breakfast cups per head
		4 qt for white coffee allowing 1 after-dinner cup per head
Tea		5/6 pts for tea
Bread: sandwiches	55-60 slices per 4 lb loaf	
toast	35 slices per 4 lb loaf	

Table of Quantities

best to arrange purchasing and storage on an *ad hoc* basis to suit the work in hand. At the other end of the scale, large catering firms will have strict purchasing and storage policies drawn up and managers charged with the responsibility of seeing they are implemented.

Patterns will change as a business grows but initially all shopping will probably be done as the orders come in. Gradually, as orders increase in regularity and size, it will make sense to bulk buy basics such as flour, sugar, tinned foods, cooking fats and oils. Then, when the firm enters the big league, and large orders are a regular event, all non-perishable goods will be bought in bulk and perishable goods bought deep frozen or delivered daily direct from the suppliers.

The choice of outlet is fairly wide. To start with, it is probably best to use a combination of supermarkets, cash and carries and small local shops. Supermarkets offer very competitive prices for branded goods in standard domestic package sizes. A number offer their own brands which will be a little bit cheaper than the well-known brands, but be careful to test the quality before buying in stocks. Special offers and loss leaders can also be picked up each week in the supermarkets, so it's important to keep your eyes open for these. However, supermarket fruit and vegetables are generally more expensive than those in the specialist greengrocers.

Cash and carry
Cash and carries can be excellent as they sell goods in large catering sizes as well as domestic packs. They are also better geared to shoppers buying in quantity: their trollies are heavy duty to take large loads, pay out desks have large conveyor belts to ease the unloading and loading of trollies, and car parks are conveniently placed so shoppers merely wheel their trollies straight out of the building to the car or van.

Cash and carries run their own special offer promotions like supermarkets and, provided storage space is not a problem, large savings can be made on these. Remember, however, to compare their prices for all goods carefully with your local supermarket prices. The name 'cash and carry' implies substantial discounts, but often prices can be the same as if not higher than those in the High Street supermarkets. Another point to bear in mind is that cash and carries are normally sited on the outskirts of town or in the country and it may be more cost effective to buy in the High Street than to spend an hour longer making a round trip to the cash and carry.

Local shops

While their prices tend to be higher, there are occasions when it makes more sense to buy from small, local shops. For instance, if an order comes in at very short notice for a small lunch or dinner party the following day, it can be better to save time and pop round the corner to the shops rather than drive to the supermarket. Similarly, if a function falls just after a bank holiday, you will probably have to buy some of the perishable ingredients, such as cream, at the last moment and again there probably won't be time to shop anywhere else but round the corner.

Markets

Markets are good places to shop whether your business is small, medium or large. Local markets are good for small businesses, while medium and larger firms will probably find it worth while to buy from the large wholesale markets. Local markets are geared to the housewife and are open normal shopping hours though some may only open for half a day or on certain days of the week. The range of goods available differs widely — some markets sell only fruit and vegetables while others deal with dairy produce, meat and fish as well. The large wholesale markets open in the small hours and are usually closed by midday. In large cities, they may specialise in a particular type of produce, as Billingsgate, Smithfield and Nine Elms (the new Covent Garden) do.

It will be important to weigh up the merits of the large discounts that can be obtained from these markets against the cost of detailing two or three members of staff to different markets at anti-social hours of the morning. Unlike supermarkets, there is no overall quality control. It is therefore vital to do a good deal of research and shop only from stalls whose quality can be relied upon. It pays dividends to build up a good relationship with the stallholders you use, letting them know that, while you are happy to buy from them exclusively, you will have no hesitation in switching should quality drop or prices rise unreasonably.

Wholesalers

An alternative to markets is to buy direct from wholesalers or, if turnover warrants it, direct from the manufacturer. In these circumstances, the supplier will normally insist on some assurance that orders will not only be large but also frequent. They will probably want some proof of your firm's creditworthiness and financial standing, too, if goods are bought on account. In turn, you will want assurance that your orders will receive prompt attention and that the delivery service is flexible enough to meet your needs. If delivery is available on a daily basis, there are obviously no problems, but if it is weekly or longer, purchasing flexibility is lost. On the plus side, orders can be placed at short notice by phone, goods will be delivered to the door and a month or so's credit is given.

Other purchasing factors

Cash flow will be a strong influence on a firm's purchasing policy. New businesses which have to lay out money in a variety of directions to get themselves going will obviously have a restricted amount of money to spend on food stocks. Gradually, as more orders come in, more funds can be allocated to bulk purchasing, thus reducing the unit cost of dishes. Established companies will be familiar with the pattern of their cash flow and should be able to use this information to their best advantage. There will, however, always be certain times of the year when cash flow is tighter than usual. For instance, August and January are quiet months in the trade and this will be reflected in reduced receipts a month or two later. It is worth reiterating the importance of establishing right from the start what payment terms to adopt. Chapter 11 deals with this in detail. Once the policy has been set, clients should be made aware of the terms and controls set up to ensure that no payments get overlooked. If accounts are not settled on time, profits start to dwindle and the client is being subsidised by the caterer. Invoices should be sent out promptly and chased up as soon as payment becomes overdue.

Shelf life is another important consideration when planning your purchasing policy. Modern technology has increased the life of numerous products with developments in preserving, canning and freezing techniques, but even so, there is a limit to the length of time any food can be stored. Retail goods have 'best before' or 'sell by' dates marked on them. Catering packs and goods from wholesalers may not indicate this information, in which case phone or write to the manufacturers asking what the shelf life is. Being aware of the life of foods is not only a guard against food poisoning, it is also a means of minimising stock wastage, which in turn means profit levels are more likely to be maintained.

Food that is in season for only a short while should be bought in bulk while prices are low provided, of course, that adequate storage facilities are available and that there is a demand for the goods. Soft fruits and vegetables are obvious examples, but there will also be fluctuations in meat and fish prices which are worth capitalising on. If you are not sure of the freezer life of any goods, there are numerous freezer books which give detailed information on this point.

Wherever a firm buys its supplies, it is vitally important that the person responsible for purchasing is experienced and competent in this field. If your company is to trade profitably you must be sure that it is buying the right quality goods at the right price and at the right time, otherwise your profits will disappear down the drain in wasted food and unnecessary expenditure.

Storage

The amount of space that is needed for storage will obviously be related to the size of your business and the turnover, but whether a business is large or small, storage space is an expensive commodity. It is, therefore, very important to make the most effective use of the existing space, even if this means a capital outlay to purchase additional shelving and storage units. It is also vital to check your storage costs on a regular basis. Increases in rent, rates, electricity, gas and salaries are edging the costs up all the time and if this increase is not taken into account, a firm cannot hope to get its general costings accurate nor achieve its planned profit levels.

As your business grows, your storage space will need to be increased. Again, this expansion should be carefully planned and calculated if it is to be cost effective. First, the existing space must be analysed: could more shelving units be added to increase space, if so what would this cost, are there any offices which could be turned over to storage, could purchasing patterns be changed to eliminate the need for more space, how costly would this be in staff time?

If the answers to these questions are negative, then it is likely you have no alternative but to find additional premises. If you are very lucky, there may be premises adjacent or nearby for purchase or rental, but if this is not the case, you will have to consider moving to larger premises altogether. Needless to say, this is an expensive exercise and should only be undertaken if there are strong indications of a sufficient upturn in trade to support the moving costs and the general increase in overheads.

Whether you are redesigning existing storage space or starting with new premises, the points to consider will be the same.

- What should the proportion of shelf storage be to fridge and freezer space?
- Is it more economic to buy shelving units and cupboards or to have these built by a carpenter?
- Do the surfaces of all units meet the hygiene regulations?

81

● Will domestic fridges and freezers be adequate or will it be necessary to buy trade units which have larger capacities and booster cooling systems for maintaining constant and precise temperatures when they are frequently being opened? Many companies offer trade discounts so remember to enquire about these and compare costs before deciding on any item.

In large store-rooms, shelving and floor stresses have to be calculated to make sure they will bear the maximum loading. There must be sufficient space between shelving and storage units for wheeling trollies and loading and unloading goods. Fridges and freezers should be on wheels so that they can be moved easily for cleaning. Shelving and cupboards should be designed for thorough and easy cleaning. Plans will need to be made for foods that have to be stored separately. Cooked and raw meats, for example, should never be stored in the same units. Pungent foods such as fish, cheeses and herbs should be stored separately so that they do not taint other items. There must be adequate ventilation and temperature controls, possibly with booster cooling facilities for hot weather.

Stocks will need to be dated and stored systematically to ensure that the oldest is always used first. Stock control systems should be set up to make re-ordering a simple procedure, and a security system established to guard against pilfering. Health officers from your local authority inspect catering premises from time to time and, if they are not satisfied with hygiene standards, they will insist on alterations being made. As these can be costly, it is worth getting things right at the planning stage, so ask your local Health Officer to come and inspect your premises and advise on the standards required. By taking such precautions, and planning and reassessing your purchasing and storage policies, you will stand a far better chance of building up a sound and healthy business than if you simply leave them to develop on their own in a rather haphazard way.

Chapter 10

Staffing

A very important factor in running a successful and profitable business is getting the staffing levels right. This applies to small firms just as much as to large ones. If a business is overstaffed, substantial sums go out every week in unnecessary wages. Added to this, output per person will often be reduced as the pressure levels are too low to create the right atmosphere of vitality and enthusiasm.

A new company is in the happy position of being able to build up its staff as the business grows. Nevertheless, it must assess the staffing needs accurately at every stage of development, otherwise over- or under-staffing will occur. Established companies need to review their staffing on a regular basis to check that they are operating at the most effective level. They must consider too whether the staffing levels and staff training policies are adequate for any planned expansion of the business.

A catering company offers a wide range of services to its clients and it must therefore employ either full- or part-time, permanent or temporary staff, who are experienced in all the different skills that these services demand. Initially, staff may have to perform a whole variety of jobs, helping out wherever necessary. As the volume of work increases, the company will be able to employ more staff, who can then concentrate on their own areas of work. Whichever the case, what sort of staff does a catering company employ?

Management

As management is concerned with the direction and coordination of work, it seems sensible to consider this aspect of staffing first. The term has rather grand connotations and implies high-powered decision makers who are remote from the practical problems and dramas of the kitchen floor. The sort of management under discussion here is, however, the very practical day-to-day management of the business.

If yours is a small business you will probably be the only manager. However, if you are operating with freelance cooks it may be that they will be responsible for both the managerial and the practical side of things. They could be asked to take care of the planning and execution from beginning to end, getting the brief from the client, drawing up menus and costings, typing the quotes, planning the work schedules, supervising the cooking, arranging the ancillary services and overseeing the function on the day. In these circumstances the qualities to look for both in yourself and in staff are:

- *Reliability.* Can they be left to work on their own conscientiously and not let the firm down at the last minute?
- *Attention to detail.* Do they have the patience to draw up all the detailed plans and schedules which are vital if the function is to go off without a hitch?
- *Flexibility.* Are they able to switch hats at a moment's notice, using their creative skills one minute to plan menus and the next turning to detailed schedule planning?
- *Self-motivation.* As supervision will be minimal, do they have the self-motivation and discipline to see projects through from start to finish, applying the maximum effort at every stage?

In larger companies the manager concentrates on seeing that each job passes smoothly from one stage to the next without becoming himself involved in the physical work. His job will entail developing effective systems and chains of communication so that each project passes from one department to the next with no duplication of effort and everyone being aware of what is going on.

Management staff on this larger more formal level demands the following qualities:

- *Organisational skills.* Do they have a flair for organisation? Are they able to think clearly and logically and not get bogged down with detail?
- *Personnel skills.* Do they have a genuine interest in people? Are they able to lead and inspire their staff with enthusiasm? Can they assess training needs and develop on-the-job training systems?
- *Planning and development.* Are they likely to be able to assess accurately future staffing levels and plan for this in advance?

Office staff

The work carried out by office staff will be the same whether the company is large or small. The actual handling may differ slightly but in the main, it is only the volume which changes. The work will entail answering the telephones, taking messages, dealing with enquiries, typing menus, letters and invoices, filing, ordering stationery and handling the mail. Petty cash and book-keeping may also fall to the office staff except in large companies where it would be handled by the accounts department.

Office staff can often feel like the poor relations of the company, remote from the more glamorous side of the business. Get them involved by keeping them up to date with the way the business is growing, tell them about the more interesting and unusual jobs that come in and relate some of the funny incidents that happen at functions. They will then begin to find their work more interesting, seeing how it links in with all the other departments. They will also begin to appreciate the importance of their own jobs, carrying out conscientiously what may before have seemed unimportant tasks.

Cooking staff

The company's reputation will obviously stand or fall

on the quality of the cooking, so the importance of employing good cooks cannot be over-emphasised. This is not to say that the cooks have to be gourmet or cordon bleu standard. What they must be is skilled in preparing the sort of food that the company specialise in.

All cooks, whether freelance, part time or full time, should undergo a rigorous test to see that they know what they are doing. The test should not only cover cooking techniques but also health and hygiene. If a cook does not appreciate the latter aspects, there is a fair chance that he or she will produce food, at some stage or another, which causes food poisoning. Smaller firms will probably only be in a position to employ ready-trained or skilled self-taught cooks. Larger companies may take in trainees who start off preparing vegetables and acting as general helpers, but are gradually schooled in all the different aspects of cooking and presentation.

Kitchen staff and store-room hands

Neither kitchen staff nor store-room hands need to be skilled as they can be trained on the job quite easily and quickly. Honesty and reliability will be the crucial factors in selecting staff for these jobs as they may well have access to food and drink of considerable value. Sometimes the jobs are filled by trainees who are keen to work their way up through the business. In other instances, they are held by people who are not ambitious and simply want a steady job which will present them with few challenges or responsibilities. In both cases, the work should be carefully supervised and checked to see that the correct standards are being maintained. In the course of their work, both kitchen staff and store-room hands may discover ways of improving existing methods and procedures. Encourage them to think about these points and pass on any ideas they have as these could save the firm money.

Drivers and porters

These tasks may fall to any member of staff if the company is small and has an 'all hands to the pumps' philosophy. But where the volume of work is great it may be necessary to employ full-time drivers and porters. Again, reliability and honesty will be important factors in selecting these staff, as they will not only be handling goods and equipment which are worth a lot of money, but they will also have strict deadlines to meet. They must be conscientious in their work particularly regarding punctuality and attendance. You cannot afford to employ anyone who is late or, even worse, fails to turn up at the last moment. Drivers and porters must also have a responsible attitude towards security procedures. They must appreciate that they are responsible for packing and delivering items with care so that no food or equipment arrives damaged or broken. Drivers must possess clean driving licences (HGV if applicable) and be capable of carrying out minor repairs and maintenance work on their vehicles.

Waiting staff

It is as important for a catering company to have good waiting staff as it is for them to employ good cooks. First, waiting staff are in the front line and clients and guests will judge the standard of the catering partly on the standard of the waiting service. They must be neat and tidy and scrupulously clean. They must possess the correct sort of clothing and be prepared to wear uniforms where necessary. Second, waiting staff who know their job and are true professionals can save the company money. They will be fast and efficient and get the work done in half the time of less skilled staff. In fact, one of the first tasks a new catering company should set itself is to find a body of first rate professional waiters, waitresses and butlers.

Waiting staff often prefer to work on a freelance basis so it will not be necessary to take on permanent staff initially. You can simply hire them on an hourly or daily basis. Remember, though, to book them as far in advance as possible, particularly around Christmas and New Year. Later on you may want to employ a nucleus of permanent waiters or waitresses and hire in extra freelance staff as and when they are needed.

How do you know how many waiters and waitresses to book for a function? This is a bit like asking, 'How long is a piece of string?' The answer will depend on a number of factors such as how long the function lasts, how many courses are to be served, what the menu is, what drinks are to be served, whether guests will arrive together or at intervals, how far the kitchens are from the function rooms, what time the rooms must be cleared by. Having said this, the following table makes a useful starting point on which to base your estimates:

Cocktails for 30	1 waitress on food
	1 butler on drinks
Finger buffet for 30 with wine	1 waitress
Finger buffet for 30 with open bar	1 waitress on food
	1 waitress on drink
Fork buffet for 30 with wine	2 waitresses
Sit-down meal for 30 with wine and coffee	3 waitresses

For large functions it is well worth employing a butler. He will be responsible for briefing the waiting staff, overseeing their work and ensuring that the service runs like clockwork. If there is a panic at any stage, he will spot this and pull staff off another area to help out until the crisis has passed. Clients rarely appreciate how hard waiting staff have to work, and they may think the caterer has over-estimated the number required and suggest reducing it. Don't let yourself be swayed, though. Remember that you have the experience and that too few staff will have catastrophic repercussions on the day.

Finding staff

The method you choose will depend on the type of staff you are looking for. The usual sources are:

Employment agencies
Good ones will do the initial sifting and, in theory,
only send along people who are suitable for the job.
They normally have a number of people on their
books so should be able to fill posts quickly. Most
agencies will supply temporary as well as permanent
staff, which can be useful if you haven't built up your
own list of freelances. The disadvantage of using an
agency is that their fees can be high and, if you are
hiring temporary staff, you probably won't know
how efficient they are until they arrive on the day.
Jobcentres offer a free job filling service and some of
their offices specialise in hotel and catering jobs.

Press advertisements
This is a cheaper method of finding staff as advertising rates are usually lower than agency fees. However, it does mean that no initial sift is done and if the
advertisement draws a large response, you may have
to sort through a lot of paperwork and do a lot of
interviewing. Advertisements can be placed either in
trade magazines or in local newspapers, most of
which run special sections for catering jobs. The copy
deadlines for trade magazines will be longer than for
local newspapers so you will have to bear this in
mind, particularly if you want staff urgently. There
is quite a skill in writing advertisements which will
attract attention and draw the right sort of response.
Study a number of advertisements before you start
to draft your own, and if you feel you need some
advice, the advertisement staff on the paper will
often be happy to help out.

Word of mouth
This is the cheapest way of finding staff as you will
not have to pay any fees at all. Another advantage is
that if you know and respect the person who makes
the recommendation, then they will be unlikely to
introduce you to anyone who is unsuitable. The disadvantage of this method is that it takes time and
will be of no use if you need to find staff quickly.

Schools and colleges
Schools and colleges can be an excellent source of staff if you are looking for people who need training or who have only just finished their training and want to gain experience. You may become involved in a lot of sifting and interviewing, but it will only cost you time.

Chapter 11
Quoting for Jobs

If you are just starting up, you will probably find pricing your services a complicated and time-consuming business, but it has to be done before you can quote for a job. The prices of ingredients will not be immediately at your fingertips and you may not be quite sure of all your overhead costs. However, things do get easier as you progress and gain in experience.

Pricing your menus

The first step is to cost thoroughly and carefully every dish on your proposed menus. You will also have to do the same for any dishes which you devise specially for a specific client. Make a list of all the ingredients in a particular dish, including the tiny amounts of things like salt, pepper, herbs and spices. Take a reasonable quantity, such as that for 12, 24, 36 people or more, depending on the type of business you are planning, and put prices against each ingredient.

This will give you a basic food cost. Add to this basic cost estimates for garnishes and decorations, fuel costs for cooking, wrappings or containers and labels. Now divide by the number of portions and this will give you a cost per head for the dish. Take care with all of this for, if you underestimate prices or overlook any items, it will mean a reduction in your profit margin. This may not amount to much on individual jobs but multiplied over the year the loss of profit could be quite significant.

The next step is to cost in your overheads. This can be done dish by dish or menu by menu. Overhead costs will include some or all of the following items:

Rent and rates
Wages
Gas, electricity and telephone, excluding cooking
    fuel
Transport
Advertising and publicity
Administration, stationery and postage
Bank loans and overdrafts
Clothing
Equipment
Insurance
Wastage
Laundry
Depreciation on capital equipment

Work out what the costs are likely to be for each month and remember to add in your own remuneration under wages. Divide the total by the number of people you expect to cater for during the same period. You now have a fixed cost which can be added to every per capita estimate of the food costs. This final sum will give you the minimum you must charge to cover all your costs and remain in business. There will, however, be many occasions when you will be able to charge more. The above figure tells you the lowest you can possibly go in any quotation. It does not include a percentage profit over and above a reasonable wage for yourself and this gives you some scope for juggling with prices.

When you have costed your menus, compare your prices with those quoted by your competitors to make sure you are not under- or over-charging. Double check all your estimates on a regular basis by comparing estimated against actual costs and profits. Initially, it will be worth doing this on a monthly basis so you can spot any shortfall at any early stage and make the necessary price adjustments.

Specific quotations

If you are sending out sample menus you should make sure that the potential customers know exactly what the prices include and what they do not. Usually, the extras include equipment hire, waiting staff, flowers and other ancillary services.

When it comes to producing a specific quotation for a particular job, it is important to make sure that all these items are included in the quotation or the client may refuse to pay for them when he gets the bill.

For jobs such as small buffets or desk-top luncheons, some of these charges may look better costed into the overall price. The delivery charge for equipment hire, for example, can push up the per capita level on small orders. This does not look so off-putting if it is included in the overall cost of the meal.

Terms

Your quotation should also clearly state your terms of business. These may be different for different types of customer. For example, you may be able to get some of the money in advance from smaller customers or from private clients. With larger business clients you may have to go for payment within 28 or even 56 days. Some firms offer a discount for prompt payment. If you do this, remember to cost the discount into your charges.

It can be quite important to quote job numbers and order references, so check that these are clearly indicated on your quotation — and again on invoices — and that the name and address are correctly typed.

Chapter 12
Cocktails and Drinks Parties

Cocktail parties seem to have come full circle and are back in fashion again, after the vogue for wine and cheese, and 'wine with nibbles'. This turn of events gives the caterer the chance once more to go to town providing creative and imaginative cocktail bits. The call for simple food still exists, of course, and may prevail depending on the area. Look carefully at your catchment area to see what the demand is likely to be. In cities or affluent parts of the country there may be a call for someone who specialises in exotic or exclusive menus. In smaller towns, the main demand may be for simpler fare or a combination of the two.

Whatever the market, it is almost certain that other caterers will be competing for the work and that the client will ask three or four companies to submit quotes. Preparing quotes is dealt with in detail in Chapter 11, but the main points to discuss with the client before drawing up menus and prices for a cocktail or drinks party are:

What is the celebration?
What time will it begin?
How long will it last?
How many guests are expected?
What age will they be?
Where will the party be held?
What floor will it be on?
Are there kitchen and cooking facilities?
What floor are these on?
Are there parking facilities?
Is the client restricted to a budget?
Is quality more important than cost?
Will glasses and other extras be required?
Will waitress service be required?

Discussing these points with the client will give you a feel for the style of food he is looking for, the sort of price he is prepared to pay, and any additional costs you are likely to incur and will need to cover, such as equipment hire or car park fees. Remember, too, that preparing cocktail snacks is fiddly and time-consuming and may not always be profitable. For large parties it is usually safe to quote on a price per head basis but for small ones of, say, 10 to 15 people this is quite uneconomic: far better to quote a flat fee plus the cost of the food and preparation.

While cocktail parties are a lot shorter than most other functions and the quantities of food only small, the range of menus is just as extensive as for dinners or buffets. For simple events, it may just be a case of buying in prepared foods such as gala pie, quiche and pizzas and cutting these up and presenting them attractively. For the more exotic parties you will need to provide an interesting and imaginative selection of individually prepared and beautifully decorated items. The time of year and the facilities available may dictate whether the food should be hot or cold. Sometimes a mixture of both is a good idea.

Special foods may be needed depending on the nationality or religion of the guests. To maintain profit margins, you may have to mix expensive and economical recipes. Consider which items will be quick and which will be time-consuming to prepare. Think of colour combinations and how the food can be presented when it is laid out on trays. Check there is a balance of meat, fish, bread, pastry and vegetables. And most important, consider how easy it will be for guests to pick up and eat each item. There are, of course, a number of old favourites which everybody loves and asks for, such as vol au vents and sausages, but generally, cocktail menus provide the caterer with a creative challenge.

Some firms send out lists from which the client selects a given number of pieces. Others prepare a selection of menus for the client to choose from. Inevitably with the latter, clients will want to incorporate at least one item from another menu or to add some particular favourite of their own. When this happens, remember to check whether the changes have affected your profit margin—it may be necessary to increase your prices. With the list method, too, clients may choose all the expensive or fiddly items and prices may need to be adjusted.

When you are preparing your menus, bear in mind what other commitments you will have at the time. If you are likely to be short-staffed or excessively busy, include items which are quick and simple or which you will be batch cooking around that time. It may sound like cheating, but this sort of streamlining will enable you to offer a higher standard of food and service in the long run. Here are some sample menus:

Simple menu using bought items
Squares of Pizza
Fingers of Gala Pie
Quarters of Scotch Egg with Mayonnaise Dip
Squares of Quiche
Sausage Rolls, cocktail size
Pâté Canapés
Mushroom Vol au Vents

Hot menu
Cocktail Sausages
Chicken Vol au Vents
Croques Monsieur
Scampi Balls with Tartar Sauce Dip
Bacon and Mushroom Rolls
Asparagus Bonnes Bouches
Tomato and Herb Pastry Pinwheels

Cold menu
Celery Boats with Smoked Trout Filling
Egg and Cress Pinwheels
Stuffed Mushrooms
Cocktail-size Salmon Sandwiches
Cream Cheese and Walnut Canapés
Curried Chicken Tartlets
Banana and Parma Ham on Cocktail Sticks

Exotic menu
Prawn and Pineapple Canapés
Camembert and Caraway Seed Circles
Spicy Meatballs with Tomato Sauce

Smoked Salmon and Avocado Canapés
Slivers of Rare Roast Beef with Stroganoff Dip
Philo Pastry Parcels with Fennel and
Broccoli Purée Filling
Cucumber Circles with Cream Cheese and
Caviar Topping

Once your client has chosen his menu and confirmed the booking, it is important to start the planning and organisation immediately. Even if the function is some months away, it is worth doing some of the groundwork at this early stage. You never know how busy you will be nearer the time and, if you're dealing with large numbers as is often the case with cocktail and drinks parties, you will need a longer run-in period. These initial plans may be no more than jottings on the file or action notes in your diary, but they will minimise the risk of your waking up one morning to find the function is only days away and nothing prepared.

Many cocktail pieces can be frozen, so if you use a freezer, an advance cooking schedule can be drawn up. Pastry cases, vol au vents and bonne bouche cases will freeze beautifully. Similarly, deep fried croûtons make excellent bases for canapés and freeze perfectly. Pizzas, flans, sausage rolls and sausages can be cooked well in advance, though the sausages will need a good wipe to remove any excess fat before freezing. Uncooked croque monsieur will freeze, leaving only the frying to be done on the day. Cocktail pieces are generally delicate, so it is important to pack and store them carefully. Plastic boxes are ideal, but if you are short of freezer space, set aside a particular area for fragile bits.

If you are not familiar with the premises where the party is to be held, it may well be worth making a recce, preferably with the client. The size of the rooms and the proximity of the kitchens may dictate the number of waitresses you need. Check the delivery point for the drink and food. This may be a long way from the kitchens and it is useful to know in advance so that you can bring extra staff to cope with the unloading. The client may have told you that there was masses of room and plenty of tables, but inspection of the premises may show that this is just not the case and that alternative arrangements may have to be made. Check, too, at what time you can have access to the rooms and whether they must be vacated by a certain time.

Depending on the time of year, you may need to book staff well in advance, so tie them up early. Christmas and New Year are obvious examples, but there will be other periods which are affected by local events such as large race meetings, golf championships, exhibitions, conferences and civic functions. Remember, too, that the better the staff the fewer you will need.

Equipment is not generally a problem for cocktail and drinks parties, as all that is usually needed is glasses, trays, ashtrays, table-cloths, corkscrews, bottle-openers and can-openers, ice buckets, tongs, jugs, plates for the garnishes and cocktail shakers. Always provide plenty of glasses, say 50 per cent more than needed, as guests may change drinks in the course of the evening or lose track of their glasses. If hot punch is being served, check the heating facilities—it may be necessary to hire a heater.

For large functions, glasses and drink may need to be delivered at different times, in which case, be sure to make security arrangements for the drink. Alcohol is a very tempting commodity and caterers have to guard against pilfering all the time. Boxes should be numbered and counted in and out by a reliable member of staff. Any drink that is being delivered in advance should be stored in a locked room or cupboard.

One of the marvellous things about most cocktail food is that it packs down small. While huge crates of food have to be carted around for large buffet parties, cocktail pieces, even for large gatherings, can be packed in a few light trays or boxes. They are, however, very fragile so will need to be packed carefully in rigid boxes. Sandwiches and bread pinwheels which have been prepared in advance will need to be well sealed in cling film—two layers may sound extravagant but it will ensure they arrive fresh and moist. Of course, the price to pay for ease of carriage is quite a long time setting up and finishing off, so allow for this.

The actual amount of work that has to be done on the day will depend on the menu. If most of the items have been pre-cooked and frozen, it will simply be a matter of making fillings and doing last-minute decorating. But some canapés may have to be put together just beforehand to prevent them from going soggy. Vegetable cases, such as tomatoes and cucumbers, can weep so will need to be filled at the last minute too. If the menu includes hot food it is helpful to work out a time schedule for the heating. And remember to allow a short cooling period so that guests don't burn their fingers or mouths.

You may not always be asked to provide the drink at cocktail parties, but there will certainly be occasions when you will need to offer this service. For detailed information on this subject, turn to Chapter 18.

Catering for cocktail and drinks parties can be both profitable and satisfying. With a little thought, the time-consuming and fiddly aspects can be tightened up and streamlined. And, for the creative caterer, they offer a wonderful opportunity to exercise his artistic talents and present some really stunning displays of food.

Chapter 13

Finger Buffets

A lot of people get confused over the actual purpose of finger buffets and tend to think of them simply as a cheap and cheerful way of providing a meal. More substantial than cocktail pieces but not as costly as a fork buffet, finger buffets are for people who 'can't afford to put on a proper spread'. In certain instances, this may be true, but more often than not you will find that there are very practical reasons for choosing a finger buffet. They are not the poor relation of catering, but a very flexible and useful way of serving food which holds its own alongside cocktail snacks and fork buffets in the list of catering alternatives.

Because of this confusion, you should always stop and think carefully when a client asks for a particular type of food. By asking a few judicial questions, you will be able to gauge whether he has chosen the right form of presentation for the function. For example, a client asking for a fork buffet may, because of limitations of space or time, be better off with a finger buffet. On the other hand, a client asking for a finger buffet may really only require snacks or tea.

Never be afraid of questioning a client's thinking and advising on another course of action. You are, after all, the expert and many of your clients will have no experience of organising a function with food and drink. They will certainly not thank you if their guests eat only half the food because a lighter meal would have been more appropriate. Nor will they appreciate paying for a substantial menu, only to find half of it is left as the guests just hadn't the time to eat more.

Advantages of finger buffets

The time factor

You may be asked to provide lunch for 200 people attending a conference. Wine and soft drinks are to be served with the meal and coffee afterwards. From the conference agenda you see that the delegates have only an hour for lunch. They will inevitably spend 10 minutes at each end of this hour stretching their legs, visiting the washrooms or simply unwinding, so the eating and drinking time is in fact only 40 minutes. Deduct another 10 minutes for delegates to queue for the main course and to return for the dessert and you will see that there would not be enough time to eat a fork buffet comfortably. If the food was presented as a finger buffet, however, delegates would need to make only one trip to the buffet table, and once there they would be able to help themselves to the food more quickly. Waitresses could circulate with trays of food, speeding up the proceedings even more and making the lunch a much more relaxed and enjoyable affair for the guests.

Alternatively, if the function is to be a long one starting, say, at noon and running on until midnight, guests will obviously need to be fed more than once. A sit-down meal at lunch time will keep people going until the evening, but by then they will need something else to keep them going through the evening. Having already served a sit-down meal, you will want to ring the changes and a running finger buffet is a sensible alternative.

The space factor

While some clients will choose premises to suit the size of their party, others will have to make do with rather smaller than ideal premises. A young couple, getting married and short of money, may have to hold the reception in their small flat. Businessmen wanting a working lunch may not have access to a large enough office to lay on a fork buffet. In such instances, the finger buffet provides the solution. The food can be laid out on a smaller table than would be required for a fork buffet or it can be handed round by waitresses and so avoid completely the need for large buffet tables.

The cost factor

Finger buffets do, of course, play a very important role when the client is restricted to a small budget. Finger food obviously has to be easy to pick up, and the most suitable food tends to be the cheaper pastry- and dough-based items. Prices can also be kept low because fewer waitresses will be needed, as there will be less laying out, clearing down and washing up to be done.

The food

If there is a drawback to finger buffets, it is that it can be difficult to think up imaginative menus. Simple buffets are obviously no problem, but it is sometimes challenging to devise interesting menus for the more sophisticated functions. The answer here is a little lateral thinking. Stop thinking in terms of conventional finger food and start thinking how other dishes can be adapted. Starters, main courses and desserts, with a little ingenuity, adaptation and scaling down can make excellent finger food. For example, spiced Italian meatballs are a good supper or lunch dish when served with buttered noodles. They can also make equally delicious finger food, served on cocktail sticks with a thicker sauce, the consistency of a dip. Similarly, lamb chops grilled with rosemary and left to cool are surprisingly tasty and very easy to eat with your fingers.

Foreign food is often a good source of new ideas. Small versions of spring rolls and samosas make excellent additions to the menu, as do skewers of pork satay or sweet and sour prawn balls. Watch out for new ideas and you'll find you have soon collected a sizeable repertoire of menus for finger buffets. Keep an eye, too, on the balance of your menus. Pastry- and dough-based items are easy to think of, but you will need meat, vegetables and sweet things to balance them and introduce variety into the menu.

Sample menus

Economical finger buffet
Fingers of Spinach Quiche
Pâté and Salad Baps
Tomato Halves filled with Spiced Rice
Bridge Rolls with Egg and Anchovy Mayonnaise
Sausage Rolls
Cheese and Pickle Sandwiches
Squares of Pizza
Mixed Vol au Vents
Slices of Treacle Tart

Businessman's working lunch
Boned Chicken Pieces baked in Egg
and Breadcrumbs
Ham Cornets filled with Cream Cheese
and Walnuts
Roast Beef and Horseradish Sandwiches
Prawn Sandwiches
Spring Rolls with Soya Dip
Seafood Tartlets
Cucumber, Melon and Tomato Kebabs
Camembert Croquettes
Individual Glazed Apricot Tartlets

Imaginative finger buffet
Salmon with Cucumber Sauce and Puff Pastry
Artichoke Heart Canapé topped with
Egg and Anchovy Mayonnaise
Marinated Pork Chops with Spicy Apple Dip
Beef Olives
Hot Cheese Fondue
Courgette with Seafood Stuffing
Croûtons topped with Chicken Livers and Grapes
Vegetable Samosas
Pineapple, Lychees, Grapes and Orange Segments
marinated in brandy and served on cocktail sticks

Hot buffet
Meat Fondue
Scampi with Tartar Sauce
Mixed Vol au Vents
Herbed Sausages
Croques Monsieur

Small Jacket Potato Halves with Cheesy Topping
Crudités in Batter
Croûtons with Bacon and Mushroom Topping
Curried Chicken Parcels

Disco buffet
Chicken Drumsticks with Devilled Sauce
Ham and Salad on Pumpernickel
Pitta Bread stuffed with Spicy Mince
Curried Meatballs on Cocktail Sticks
Tomatoes stuffed with Tuna Fish Mayonnaise
Salami and Salad Open Sandwiches
Cheese, Tomato and Anchovy Quiche
Chocolate Brownies with Fudge Topping

Planning and organisation for finger buffets will be very much the same as for cocktail parties, though there will be a few differences. Preparation time will often be shorter than for cocktail pieces as the food is less delicate and fiddly to prepare. It is much quicker to make a number of large quiches and then cut these into slices for a finger buffet than it is to make the equivalent number of individual tartlets for cocktails.

You will, however, need to offer a slightly larger choice of food than for cocktail menus and often a sweet item will have to be included. Equipment will be the same, with the addition of small plates for guests to place their food on. More trays and meat flats will be needed for laying out the food and it is worth preparing labels, particularly if there won't be any waitresses around to explain what things are. It's not always easy to tell what sort of filling a sandwich has just by looking at it, and people do like to know what they are eating.

If the food has only to be laid out in advance and cleared away afterwards, few staff will be needed on the day. When there is a shortage of space, however, it may be a good idea to provide staff to replenish and tidy up the trays throughout the course of the party. With this system you need only put out a little food at a time, thus saving on the amount of space you have to give over to the buffet. Hot buffets will obviously entail more staff. Draw up time schedules for heating the food and remember to stagger the service, as if all the hot food is laid out at once, much of it will go cold before the guests get to it.

The choice of menu will dictate how much work there will be to do on the day. A lot of finger food can be prepared in advance: sandwiches with drier fillings can be made the day before and stored in the fridge overnight, well sealed in cling film. Pastry- and dough-based foods with moist fillings will have to be left to the last moment. If the food has to stand for some time before it is eaten, you will need to consider whether the room temperature will affect any of it — aspic coated foods and mousses are two classic examples of potential disaster areas. And all sandwiches will have to be left in their cling film and unwrapped at the last minute.

Chapter 14
Fork Buffets

A fork buffet can mean anything from a simple gala pie salad followed by trifle, to tables of traditional fare, an array of curries, a spread of vegetarian dishes or a selection of the finest *haute cuisine* dishes.

Because they are less formal than sit-down meals, there are many instances when fork buffets are the best way of serving food. For instance, a full sit-down meal may be too lavish and quite inappropriate for the occasion—say, when a charity or a government body is entertaining. Other times, there may be insufficient space to seat all the guests, or the host may want his guests to circulate as is often the case with the larger business functions. Time may be short, not permitting the host to seat his guests for a lengthy three course spread. Or it may be that funds simply will not stretch to a sit-down meal with all the trimmings and hire charges.

For the caterer, fork buffets can entail more work than finger buffets, both in the planning stages and in the physical work on the day. They are not, however, as demanding as sit-down meals, so should not worry the small firm or anyone just starting up in business. Fork buffets can be put together at quite short notice, as the food need not be fiddly, and the tableware, equipment and staffing need not be extensive or complicated to arrange. Some companies specialise in fork buffets and nothing else, taking on quite small functions as well as the large wedding and business parties.

For small functions, it may be necessary to make a delivery charge or ask the client to collect the food himself as the profit margin will be small. At the other end of the scale, if the function is a really large one, the caterer will often give discounts on the price per head.

The size and formality of the function will dictate how much detail you need to obtain from the client when he asks you to quote for the job. The two checklists below illustrate the great difference between items to check for a small and a large reception:

Christening party for 20 people

Number of guests — how many of these are children?
Any particular likes or dislikes in food?
Does client have hot or cold food in mind, or a
  mixture?
Discuss styles of food from plain to fancy.
Is waitress service required?
What time will the party start?
How long will it last?
Does the client want a quote for a christening cake?
What equipment will need to be hired?
Special christening napkins or printed book
  matches?
Does client have a price in mind?
Is drink required — wines, sherries, spirits,
  champagnes, liqueurs, soft drinks, fruit juices?

Anniversary party for 150 people

Number of guests — how many of these are children?
Nationality and religion of guests?
Where is reception being held?
If indoors, what floor will it be held on?
If in a marquee, will there be electricity and
  water supply?
Will drink be required?
If so, will this be a full bar or just sherries and
  wines?
Is champagne required for the toasts?
Will coffee and tea be required at the end of the
  meal?
What time will the married couple arrive?
When will the buffet start?
How many speeches will there be and how long will
  they last?
Would the client like a quote for the cake?

107

Hire requirements: crockery, cutlery, glass—sherry,
   wine, spirits, champagne, tables, table-cloths,
   cakestand and knife, ice buckets.
Are table decorations and flower arrangements
   required?
Does client have any firm ideas for the menu?
Discuss different styles of food.
Should menu be hot, cold or a mixture of both?
Does client have a budget in mind?
What are the storage facilities on site for
   equipment and drink?
What is the security like?
Are there parking facilities?

Though thick steaks and all other foods that need
cutting up are generally unsuitable there is, on the
whole, a wide range of standard main course dishes
which will be perfect for the fork buffet. Cold dishes
may seem to pose a problem at first, as recipe books
often don't feature many of these. However, many
hot dishes are equally delicious when served cold. Try
out a few and you will soon get a feeling for which
ones adapt well.

   Foreign dishes also make excellent fork buffet
dishes and many of these can be served cold as well as
hot. The kitchen facilities on site may influence the
menu planning—for instance, if there are not enough
fridges on site, salmon mousse would be inappropriate on a menu for 150 people. The room temperature
may also affect the choice of food, especially if it has
to be laid out well in advance—will the aspic coatings
melt and the salads go limp before the guests arrive?
If the numbers are large, go for dishes that are quick
to serve rather than those that are fiddly to dish up or
take time to carve. There is nothing more irritating
than to queue up for a long time waiting to be served.
With these points in mind, some sample menus are
given. Several offer a selection of main courses. This
is because people love to taste a little bit of a number
of tempting dishes. With buffets for very small numbers it would be quite uneconomical to offer this
selection.

Sample menus

Hot fork buffet for 20 or more
Coq au Vin
Lamb à la Grècque
Boeuf à la Bourgignonne served with Brown Rice
with Caraway Seeds, French Beans tossed in
Butter and sprinkled with Toasted Almonds
and Buttered Baby Carrots
Coffee Meringue Gateau
Caramelised Oranges

Cold buffet for large numbers
Chicken Galantine with Spiced Apricots
Slices of Rare Roast Beef with Horseradish Sauce
Spicy Paella served with Potato and Chive Salad,
Tomato and Anchovy Salad, Caesar Salad, Coleslaw
Tarte au Pommes
Hazelnut Meringue Cake

Business lunch for 20
Smoked Salmon Mousse
Cold Beef Stroganoff served with Brown Rice
Salad, Green Salad and Avocado and Tomato Salad
Profiteroles
Coffee and Walnut Mousse

Anniversary party buffet for 150
Melon, Cucumber and Tomato Cocktail
Cold Salmon and Hollandaise Sauce served with
New Potatoes tossed in French Dressing,
Cucumber and Dill Salad, Stuffed Tomatoes
and Green Salad
Apple and Orange Charlotte
Raspberry Meringue Cake

Advance planning

Even if the buffet is a small one you will want to prepare a work schedule as soon as the order is confirmed. In fact, it's worth doing one in your head
when you are first asked to quote just to check that
your order book is not too full and that you can
accommodate the work. It is better to turn down the
odd job rather than take on more than you can handle

and run the risk of damaging your reputation with a lower standard of food and service. Turning down work is never easy, but remember that it can sometimes enhance your reputation, as clients will assume you must be good if you are that busy and the word will get round that you have to be booked well in advance.

First study your menu and see how much can be prepared in advance. Can any of it be linked with any batch cooking you will be doing for other functions? Make a note of the foods that will have to be prepared at the last moment. Some salads will fall into this category, though remember that things like pasta and rice salad can be cooked in advance, frozen and then dressed on the day. Many salads will keep well for a day or two in the fridge which means you will be able to stagger your last minute work load over two or three days. Check that there will be sufficient space in the fridges, though. Think about the sauces, dressings and garnishes. Which of these can be prepared in advance and which will have to be left to the last moment?

Work out a buying plan along the same lines as the work schedule. At certain times, some foods may be in short supply or in great demand, so you will want to order them well in advance; salmon around Wimbledon and Ascot, for instance, and strawberries in winter. Staff will need to be booked but, if the lead time to the function is too long, make a diary note to do this later on.

What equipment will you need to order? This will probably be no more than dinner plates and forks, dessert plates and spoons, glasses and perhaps some tableware, such as condiment sets and dishes. Specify whether the cutlery should be stainless steel or silver plate—there is a considerable difference in the price. Always order more crockery and glass than is necessary in case extra guests arrive unexpectedly or there are accidents in the kitchen. If the buffet is hot and the kitchen facilities poor, remember to order cookers, water heaters, and in really bad cases, you may even have to hire tables to work from.

If the function is a small one, the delivery arrangements will be quite simple, but if it is large these will need to be worked out carefully. Consider which articles are fragile and will need to be packed separately. Think about how heavy the crates and boxes of food will be and how many staff will be needed to load and unload these. If you haven't enough van space yourself, it may be necessary to hire some transport, whether this be a willing taxi firm or a van hire company. Your drink and equipment suppliers will probably deliver direct to the site, so bear this in mind when you are estimating how much car space you will need. If any items are delivered direct, make sure they are checked off and signed for, either by someone on site who is prepared to take responsibility for them or by a member of your staff.

Book up any ancillary services such as flower arrangements, toast-masters and novelty printing for book matches or paper napkins, and make sure that all are given thorough briefs on what is required. With printed items, remember to leave enough time for proofs to be prepared and approved.

Work on the day

While the smaller functions will only require a couple of hours 'setting up' time, it will be necessary to arrive and start work much earlier for large functions. The work will be more or less the same, but there will obviously be much more of it when the guest list runs into hundreds rather than twenties. For large functions, it is vital that the day starts with a staff briefing so that everyone knows exactly what to do and no tasks are duplicated or overlooked. The main tasks will be:

Cooking or reheating the food.
Laying the buffet table.
Polishing the cutlery and glass.
Checking and polishing crockery.
Arranging food on serving dishes.
Decorating and garnishing.
Setting up the bar.
Preparing tea and coffee trays.

There will doubtless be a series of unforeseen tasks—

the host may arrive with a box of oranges which he would like squeezed and served as fresh juice. Some vital piece of equipment may have been left behind and a member of staff have to be despatched to collect it or get hold of another one locally.

Although the laying up of the table will be simple in that it will not include place settings with numerous knives, forks and spoons, it must still be done carefully. The table-cloths must all reach down to the floor and the corners should be tucked and pinned. This not only makes them look smart but also stops people tripping over the loose ends. All the cutlery must be polished and the crockery must be wiped and checked for cracks and chips. Forks and spoons must be neatly arranged—it's a good idea to roll them in napkins and then stack them in an attractive pattern at the end of the table, preferably the far end.

Thought should be given to traffic flow as this will dictate which end of the table guests will start from. For very large functions there may be a case for having a number of separate buffet tables dotted round the room rather than one long table. This will help speed up the serving and avoid a build-up of people waiting to be served. Alternatively, use both sides of the buffet table or make two access points on one side. The bar should be positioned to help the traffic flow around the room, too. Glasses should be arranged in an attractive pattern and the drinks laid out for ease of service. Check that all the bar tools have been delivered: corkscrews, can- and bottle-openers, sharp knife, swizzle stick, cocktail shaker, ice and ice-buckets, white cloths, lemon and orange slices, cherries, olives and cocktail sticks. Spare glasses and drink can be kept under the table so the staff don't have to go rushing off to restock half-way through the party. Remember, too, to put a few large rubbish boxes or bags under the bar and buffet tables.

If the menu is hot there will be a lot of activity in the kitchens. Test all the equipment on arrival to see that it works and remember to allow time for the heaters and cookers to heat up. Large water heaters, for instance, can take up to an hour to come to the boil and if these haven't been switched on in time, the coffee could be a disaster. Check all the food and arrange it systematically on the work surfaces to minimise the amount of running around that has to be done. See that everyone is familiar with the cooking and serving schedules. Tray up the coffee cups and saucers and stack these ready for use.

Chapter 15
Sit-down Meals

A sit-down meal can cover anything from an intimate dinner party for six to a formal banquet for hundreds of people, but whether the function is large or small, the demands on the caterer and his staff will be far greater than for buffets or cocktail parties. To begin with, there will be an increase in the number of courses on the menu. While buffet menus are normally two, occasionally three courses, the sit-down meal will have three, four and sometimes five courses. It is unusual to have a cold main course so at least one and often two will be hot. You will need staff who are skilled in silver service and can work quickly and quietly, often under extremely difficult conditions. The overall numbers will obviously dictate just how taxing a sit-down function will be.

Sit-down meals for up to 20 people

These will normally be business lunches or private dinner parties. While large catering companies will accept small jobs like these, there is a large army of freelance cooks or small catering companies who make this area of work their major source of income. Some cooks will be employed by a company to cook lunch for the directors on a Monday to Friday basis. This provides the cook with a basic income and, because the hours are short, leaves him or her free to take on a fair amount of freelance work on top. Others will be on the books of a cooking agency and go to firms to help out when the regular cook is ill or on holiday. Here again the hours are short and the cooks boost their salaries with freelance work. Alternatively, a cook may operate totally independently, working only for her own clients.

Cooking on this scale has become extremely fashionable over the past few years and hence there is hot competition for work. Building up a book of regular clients can be a slow process, but if you are good, your reputation will spread and you should soon have a regular supply of work. Personal contacts are obviously a tremendous help in getting business, but if you are short of these, try writing to different companies telling them about your service and enclosing some sample menus.

For the dinner party market, have a leaflet printed with sample menus and have it delivered door to door to selected roads in your catchment area. There are agencies who will carry out this sort of work, but your local Boy Scouts organisation should also be happy to help out in return for a contribution to their funds. Advertisements in local newspapers, news sheets and magazines will be another way of spreading your name about and drumming up business. This is dealt with in Chapter 19.

Catering for very small parties, say two or four people, will be quite uneconomic unless you charge a flat fee plus the cost of the food. On a price per head basis, it would be very difficult to cover your costs for such small numbers. For larger parties you can charge on either basis, but do watch the costing carefully. It is very easy simply to charge for the food and forget about all the hours you have put in. When you are first starting up, and particularly with clients who are personal contacts or friends, it will be very tempting to lower your prices to attract business. While this might be a good idea short term, in the long run it will prove a disastrous policy. Your clients will become accustomed to your price range and will not readily accept any sudden increase.

Even with a small party, you will need to get a good brief from your client if you are to get the tone of the menu and service right. The sort of points you will want to cover are:

How many guests will there be?
Will their religion or nationality affect the menu?
Is it a business function or for pleasure?

What time will the guests arrive?

Will they be coming on from anywhere where they might have had cocktail snacks?

What time will they start to eat?

What time will they finish?

Should the food be plain or fancy?

How many courses should there be?

Does the host want to impress?

Is the budget limited?

Have the guests been entertained recently, if so what did they eat?

Is waitress/butler service required?

Does the client have crockery, cutlery, glasses and serving dishes?

What cooking facilities are there?

Are table decorations required?

For the small caterer, equipment can be a problem if he or she is asked to provide lunch in an office where there are no kitchen facilities or stocks of china and glass. The crockery and cutlery can, of course, be hired for a fairly reasonable sum, but it becomes very expensive if you have to start hiring portable cookers and could put you out of the running when it comes to quoting against other larger caterers who have their own equipment. There are a number of portable cookers on the market which are not too expensive to buy and may be worth investing in. When they are not in use on a job, they make very useful additional ovens in the caterer's own kitchen.

A small dinner or lunch won't present any problems for a good waitress who is trained in silver service. But if for some reason you have to call on a waitress you have never used before, check that she is silver-serviced trained. A good waitress will also take pride in laying the table correctly, though you should always check this yourself before the guests arrive. Turning this rule around, a completely novice caterer will learn a tremendous amount by watching how the waitress sets the table and presents and serves the food. In fact, finding a really professional waitress is probably one of the most important and earliest tasks a caterer should set himself. If the function is in the evening, you may need to cost in evening rates of pay for staff, and travelling costs will rise if they have to go home late at night and therefore take taxis.

One of the problems with small sit-down meals is that they never start on time. With a business lunch, the morning meeting or preceding talk always seems to overrun, and with private dinner parties there is always at least one guest who gets delayed. It is, therefore, useful to bear this point in mind when you are planning menus and working out the fine tuning of the cooking schedule. Trying to keep food warm in an unfamiliar oven is not easy, so dishes which are prepared at the last moment are often the answer.

The small sit-down meal gives the caterer the opportunity to do some of the more testing dishes which he would not dare to tackle for vast numbers of people: dishes that need quick, last minute preparation or ones with spectacular sauces. Some examples of these, along with plainer dishes, are set out in the menu section at the end of this chapter.

Sit-down meals for up to 100 people

On this scale, the numbers are still sufficiently low for the freelance cook to be able to tackle, yet at the same time they are large enough to make the exercise financially interesting for the bigger companies. The latter will have an advantage when it comes to competitive quoting as they will not have to buy in so many services. On the other hand, some clients prefer to pay a little more for the personal attention and quality of service which they get from a small firm.

One word of warning though: while the financial returns may be extremely tempting, the novice caterer would be well advised to avoid this size of function until he has built up a bit of experience. Providing sit-down meals for large numbers is in a different league from catering for buffets, with more problems and pitfalls. By taking on this sort of work too early, you may well have a disaster which will seriously damage your self-confidence. Far better to help out at one or two large functions first and then, when you know the ropes, start tendering for this type of work yourself.

Much of the work for medium-scale sit-down meals will be for Christmas parties, conferences, weddings, club dinners and other local gatherings. While personal contacts may bring in a few jobs, most of your work will be generated by placing advertisements in local newspapers. If you advertise at the right time of year, the response will probably be quite large but remember, it is the conversion of enquiries into firm orders that counts. Keep up-to-date copies of your competitors' brochures and price-lists so you know what the going rates are. Another good source of finding work is the town hall. There is normally a bulletin board in the entertainments section where you can display a small poster or card.

You will, of course, need a good briefing session with the prospective client at the premises when you can cover the following points:

Number of guests.
Purpose of the function.
Will the function have a theme?
Will religion or nationality influence the menu?
What time will the guests arrive?
What drinks will be served before the meal?
Should canapés be served too?
What style of food is required?
Are there any budget restrictions?
What time will guests sit down to eat?
What time will they finish?
Will there be speeches, if so how many and for how long?
Is a toast-master required?
Will floral arrangements/table decorations/ novelties or any other ancillary services be required?
Will there be a seating plan?
Will all the drinks be paid for by the host or will guests have to buy any or all of them?
What kitchen facilities and equipment are there?
Where are delivery points and lifts?
Will the function room seat the number of guests expected?

This information will not only be vital in helping you

get your costing right but it will also be the basis for your planning and organisation.

Menu planning is the next stage and here you will want to consider, not only the wishes of the client, but also any constraints of space, facilities or time that you have discovered in the course of your briefing. For instance, are the heating facilities sufficient to enable you to provide two hot courses or will you have to restrict this to one? Will you have to choose dishes that can be plated up at the last minute because there is insufficient space to do this in advance? If guests are likely to be late sitting down to eat, would it be better to choose a starter that will stand well? Similarly, you should consider any constraints within your own firm that may affect the menu. Will you be cooking the food in-house or will you buy it in from a supplier?

You are now in a position to work out your costings and, needless to say, it is vitally important that you get these absolutely right—particularly when you are catering for large numbers. Underestimating the cost of any item or service could turn your profits into losses. Check and recheck the costs of hire, food, staff, transportation, drink, flowers, incidentals and general overheads.

Finally, check that you have considered economies of scale and that you will make the same rate of profit if the numbers are reduced or increased, as often happens. For instance, if you cost out crockery and cutlery hire for 60 people and the numbers are increased by 10, you may find that your supplier only hires out in batches of 20 and you would be left paying for 10 settings that would not be used. If you are aware of this problem right at the start you can explain to the client why the hire charge for the extra 10 will be proportionally higher. If the problem dawns on you when you are invoicing the client, it is too late to do anything about recouping the money.

Large-scale sit-down meals

Functions for several hundred guests are really out of the scope of the small caterer, unless he or she acts purely as a coordinator, buying in the services of other companies. For the most part, large-scale catering of this nature is the domain of the medium and large catering companies.

Much of the work will be for one-off functions where the caterer is briefed for a particular job for which he produces a quote. There is, however, a great deal of contract work where a caterer will tender for the catering rights to a suite of function rooms or for the catering contract for a large company with several dining-rooms or offices. Companies may be invited to tender for a specific job or contract, but if they are keen on getting into this area of the market, they will also need to approach clients themselves and ask to be invited to tender for any future work. In the case of contract work, clients will want to know as much about the catering company as the catering company will want to know about the client—there is, after all, a great deal of money at stake. They will want to look into the caterer's systems of quality control, hygiene, storage, staff training, financing, accounting, performance and reliability. The catering company, for its part, will need a very detailed briefing from the client on the number and type of functions which it will be required to cater for over a given period, including any estimated increase or fall off in demand. Both sides have a lot to lose, so the groundwork before tendering and accepting must be done thoroughly.

Once you have been awarded the contract, the work will need to be planned like a military campaign. A work schedule should be drawn up and one member of staff made responsible for seeing that things progress on time. A typical work schedule would include the following headings:

Purchase and preparation of food
Purchase of drink
Heavy equipment
Cutlery, crockery, glass, table and service ware
Staffing
Storage
Transport

Security
Finance and accounting

Regular progress meetings between the people responsible for these tasks keep people on their toes and also often reveal the odd oversight in planning. Strict financial control will need to be maintained throughout the exercise to see that budgets are not exceeded.

Sample menus

Business lunch for 20
Chicken Liver Pâté with Brandy and Walnuts
Carré d'Agneau with Duchess Potatoes,
Brussels Sprouts and Beans
Home-made Blackcurrant Ice Cream
Cheeseboard

Dinner party for eight
Stuffed Mushrooms
Lamb Persillée en Croûte with Buttered Carrots
and French Beans
Walnut Salad
Crèpe Suzette
Cheeseboard

Rotary dinner for 100
Melon and Prawn Cocktail
Roast Beef with Roast Potatoes, Carrots
and Broccoli
Pear and Walnut Pie with Cream
Cheeseboard

Banquet for 400
Iced Beef Consommé
Smoked Mackerel with Horseradish Cream
Veal Cordon Bleu with Croquette Potatoes,
Braised Celery and Petits Pois
Raspberry Pavlova Cake
Cheeseboard

Chapter 16
Special Events

One of the joys of catering is the tremendous variety of the work. There simply isn't the chance to get bored, and creative and artistic people will find endless scope for using their talents. Engagement parties, weddings, christenings, children's parties, picnics, barbecues, halloween parties, the list goes on and on. As no two jobs will be the same, this chapter does not analyse each type of function in detail; instead it sketches the basic elements, looks at the pitfalls you may encounter and gives a few tips and ideas.

Engagement parties

Don't be surprised if you find the conversion rate of enquiries to actual orders is low. This does not necessarily mean that your prices or menus are off the mark. It very often happens that the client gets carried away with the excitement of the engagement and thinks he will get caterers in to take care of everything. By the time the quotes arrive he has begun to realise how expensive the actual wedding is going to be, with photography, flowers, dresses, car hire etc, and so decides he will save a bit of money and get the family to provide the engagement party.

Engagement parties are usually cocktails or fork buffets. They tend to be informal events where the main idea is for the engaged couple, their family and friends, to circulate and meet each other. At some stage of the reception there may be a speech or two and some toasts. Some clients may want an engagement cake served after the toasts and you may be asked to provide this. Engagement parties are usually held in the home of the bride's or groom's parents or some other member of the family, so you may find that the space and size of the rooms dictate the kind of food that is served.

As always, the key to success is the briefing and the main points you will need to discuss are:

Drinks   —soft and alcoholic
champagne or sparkling wine for the toasts

Food   —cocktail snacks, finger or fork buffet
plain or celebratory engagement cake

Staff   —waiters, waitresses, butlers

Decorations —flower arrangements
table decorations
engagement napkins and book matches

Photography —is a professional photographer required?

Timing   —start
finish
when will speeches be made?

Budget   —does client have a figure in mind?

The sort of menus you might then arrive at are:

Cocktail menu
Cheese Sables
Chicken Livers in Bacon
Asparagus Rolls
Cocktail Sausages
Small Tongue Sandwiches
Small Savoury Scones with Pizzaiola Topping
Mixed Canapés

Drinks
Mixed bar
(No speeches or toasts)

★

Fork buffet
Smoked Trout Mousse with Mousseline Sauce
Honey Roast Lamb on the Bone
Baron of Beef

Selection of Six Salads
Crème Brulée
Blackcurrant Ice Cream with Blackcurrant Sauce

Drinks
Wine, Red and White
Soft Drinks
Sparkling Wine (for speeches)

Weddings

Wedding parties can range from the simplest drinks reception with cocktail snacks through more substantial finger and fork buffets to a full sit-down meal. They may last just a couple of hours or go on through the day, ending up with a dance or disco in the evening. Sometimes they may be split, with a small family wedding breakfast in the day, followed by a large reception in the evening. The caterer may simply be called on to provide the food and drink. On the other hand, the client may want everything arranged—photography, flowers, car hire and so on.

The client usually has a basic idea of what sort of reception he wants, but on closer inspection of the costs involved it may be that his plans have to be tailored down or rethought to suit the budget. It is therefore a good idea to start off by sending a variety of menus so that he realises you can provide cheaper meals as well. The following examples cover a useful range of styles and price ranges of food:

Wedding cocktail snacks
Scampi with Tartar Dip
Walnut and Cream Cheese Rolls
Mixed Vol au Vents
Prawn Baskets
Curried Chicken Tartlets
Egg and Anchovy Canapés
Crudités with Thousand Island Dip

Formal sit-down wedding breakfast
Oeufs en Cocottes
Lamb Cutlets en Cuirasse with Duchess Potatoes
and Broccoli

Cheeseboard
Damson Mousse

Simple fork buffet for weddings
Chicken Galantine
Cold Home-cooked Tongue
Honey Glazed Ham Served with four Salads
Almond Trifle
Fresh Fruit Salad and Cream

Summer wedding—
buffet with seating arrangements
Poached Salmon
Cold Beef en Croûte Served with Potato and
Chive Salad, Cucumber Mousse, Avocado and
Walnut Salad, Green Salad, Tomato and
Melon Salad
Raspberries and Cream
Cheeseboard

The briefing meeting will be extremely important as
there will be many details to discuss. The following
checklist is designed for both large and small receptions, though you may find you can delete some of the
questions for simple functions:

How many guests will there be?
Where will the reception be held?
How big are the rooms?
What are the kitchen facilities like?
Should there be waitress service?
How long will the reception last?
Should it be a sit-down meal, a finger or fork buffet
   or cocktail snacks?
What sort of food does the client have in mind—
   simple or exotic, traditional or continental?
Will you be asked to provide the drink?
If so, what sort—sherries, wine, champagne, full
   bar, soft drinks and fruit juices?
Will crockery, cutlery and glassware have to be
   hired?
Are there sufficient tables and chairs or will these
   have to be hired?
Will you be called on to provide any ancillary
   services—flower arrangements, bouquets and

buttonholes, transport, a toast-master, photography (still and video), wedding cake?

Once you have sorted these points out you will have a good idea of the work load, and you should check this out with your order book to see whether you need to call in extra staff to help out. The majority of weddings are held from May to September so it is quite likely you will be very busy, particularly if you specialise in weddings.

Christenings

Most people arrange the catering for christenings themselves and caterers are called in when the family feel they really can't cope with the new baby as well as the food, or when the party is a large one. Normally, the christening party is a morning or tea-time finger buffet with alcohol and, of course, the christening cake. Larger christening parties are usually lunch-time or evening affairs with either cocktails or a finger or fork buffet.

By its nature, the christening party guest list embraces all age groups from toddlers to grannies and this enormous range in tastes must be borne in mind when planning the menu and drinks: soft drinks for the children, tea and coffee for the older generation; novelties such as tiny chocolate cakes in the shape of hedgehogs and mice; perennial favourites like hot sausages, smoked salmon rolls and vol au vents that will appeal to everyone. Remember to find out how many children there will be as this will affect the amount of food needed and the pricing—most caterers offer reduced prices for small children.

You may have to hire equipment if the party is a large one: hot water heaters, tea and coffee cups, glasses and small plates for a finger buffet. Dinner plates and forks, dessert bowls and spoons for the fork buffet, plus crockery and glass for the beverages and drink. If there are toasts, sparkling wine or champagne will be needed with the appropriate glasses. If the cake is to be a centre-piece, a cake stand and knife too. You may also have to supply special christening napkins and small boxes for sending bits of cake to absent family and friends. It is traditional to save the top layer of the wedding cake for the first christening, but for subsequent christenings the parents may decide to ring the changes and plump for something quite different from the traditional fruit cake with royal icing—an elaborately decorated sponge cake, an ice cream gateau or a meringue cake filled with raspberries and cream.

Christening tea
Salmon and Cucumber Sandwiches
Egg Mayonnaise Sandwiches
Tomato Sandwiches
Malt Bread, Sliced and Buttered
Sausages with Mustard Dip
Butterfly Cakes
Home-made Biscuits
Mocha Sponge Cakes with Chocolate Icing
Tea, Soft Drinks and Sherry

Christening buffet
Breaded Chicken Pieces
Croques Monsieur
Bacon Savouries
Hot Sausage Rolls
Egg and Smoked Salmon Canapés
Pâté Tartlets
Scampi on Sticks
Ham and Asparagus Rolls
Christening Cake
Wine and Soft Drinks
Champagne for the Toast

Anniversaries

Silver and golden wedding anniversaries immediately spring to mind, but there are in fact many more, such as pearl, ruby, sapphire and emerald, which you may be asked to cater for.

Some anniversary parties will be organised by the couple themselves, others will be surprise affairs arranged by the children or close friends. There is no traditional time or format for the celebrations though there is normally an anniversary cake and champagne or sparkling wine for the toasts. If the client has no fixed ideas about the sort of party he wants, find out how much money he wants to spend, how many guests there will be and how long the party will last.

From this information you can gauge what sort of function would be the most appropriate and guide the client in this direction. When the clients are elderly they may find the organising is too much for them to cope with, and you may be called on to arrange the function from start to finish. Anniversary menus will be similar to those used for weddings, but you may be asked to link the menu to a theme. Apart from the obvious 'age' theme, there may be other aspects of the couple's life that are fun to focus on: golf, music, sailing, DIY—all sorts of interests that can be featured in the cake and food, the decorations and the flowers.

Sample menus

Golden Wedding sit-down meal
Coquilles St Jacques
Roast Veal with Apricot Stuffing,
Croquette Potatoes, Fried Chicory and Peas
Lemon Parfait or Home-made Coffee Ice Cream

Silver wedding cocktail pieces
Chicken Liver Canapés
Devils on Horseback
Celery Boats Filled with Taramasalata
Cucumber Boats Filled with Smoked Trout Mousse
Camembert Crescents
Crab Pyramids
Savoury Stuffed Dates
Bacon with Water Chestnuts

Children's parties

On the surface, children's parties may appear to be quite simple affairs—they can in fact involve quite a lot of creative thought and detailed organisation.

Children's tastes are much more sophisticated than they were 20 years ago, with the emphasis on savoury items rather than the sweets and jellies of yesteryear. You will obviously have to put forward ideas for the menus but check with the mother first what sort of food the child likes, as children have pretty firm ideas about what they want. The choice of foods will depend largely on the age of the children, but here are some menus for toddlers and young children.

Sample menus

Children's birthday party
Mixed Sandwich Boat
Individual Quiches
Sausages on Sticks
Brighton French Bread Marina
Individual Fruit Jellies
Ice Cream Clowns
Steam Engine Cake

Children's Christmas party
Christmas Drumsticks
Pastry Parcels
Savoury Yule Logs
Sausage Cannon
Mince Pies
Ice Cream Snowmen
Santa Christmas Cake

Themes have changed too. Whereas the cakes used to reflect traditional topics such as trains, animals and nursery rhymes, film characters, computerised toys and sports and pop stars are the things that appeal to children today. Children's Christmas parties have changed less and the traditional foods and themes still stand—yule logs, cakes in the shape of Father Christmas, Christmas stockings, Christmas trees and reindeer.

Entertainers have stood the test of time, too (probably because they take the pressure off the parents and help to preserve their sanity) so there is still a call for conjurors, Father Christmases, balloon men, story-tellers and puppet shows, any of which you may be called on to book. Then there is the endless list of novelty items that children love: hats, masks, napkins, streamers, whistles, crackers, snowballs, lucky dips, jokes, balloons and so on. You may be asked to provide these so it is useful to trace your nearest supplier.

The problem with children's parties is that the parents often don't appreciate the time and effort that goes into preparing and presenting the food and they consider the caterer's charges excessive. They feel that because children are small, the cost of the party should be low. Don't be tempted to cut your prices though, and be particularly careful to cost in all your staff time when you are preparing your estimates, otherwise you will find you are working very hard for little or no profit.

Picnics

Picnic hampers are a creative and rewarding area of catering. They are usually wanted for special occasions such as a trip to Glyndebourne or a day at the races, so both the presentation and the food can be lavish.

Caterers who specialise in the work tend to have a range of hamper menus from which the client can choose. If you only get occasional orders for hampers, you will probably plan each menu individually. Whichever the case, you will want a clear brief from the client and the sort of things you should discuss with him are:

How many courses should there be?
Any favourite dishes to be included?
Should menu be finger or fork food?
Cutlery, crockery and glass—would client like
    disposable or not?
Table-cloths and napkins—would client like
    disposable or cloth?
Hamper—traditional basket, open basket,
    wooden box, cardboard box?
Colour schemes—any particular choice?

Drinks—wines, spirits, beers, liqueurs, port, sherry, soft drinks, coffee, tea, any others?

Once the menu has been settled, give some serious thought to how it will be presented within the hamper. The secret of a really attractive hamper is attention to detail—think how even the smallest and most insignificant items can be presented. For example:

- Tie the corkscrew, tin opener and swizzle sticks to inside of hamper lid with brightly coloured ribbons.
- Wrap cutlery in frilly doilies and tie with coloured ribbon like a posy of flowers.
- Put salt and pepper in brightly coloured paper twists.
- Present the cheeses in a mini hamper of their own.
- Carry the colour scheme through everything— the table-cloth, napkins and crockery.
- As an alternative to bowls, serve the starter in crab or scallop shells and the dessert in scooped-out grapefruit or pineapples.
- Fix a menu card to the inside lid of the hamper.

These are just a few suggestions. Think of more so that your hampers are a delight to look at as well as to eat.

There are two golden rules that must be mentioned before looking at ideas for hamper menus. First, be absolutely certain that all food and drink is carefully packed and thoroughly sealed so that nothing gets squashed out of recognition and there are no leakages. A soggy hamper with spilt or damaged food will be a disaster and ruin your client's day. Second, make sure nothing is omitted at the packing stage—a hamper with fine wines is no good if you have forgotten to put in the corkscrew or glasses! Draw up a detailed packing list and check this religiously before the hamper is delivered or collected. Your checklist will probably include most of the following:

Crockery	Menu card
Cutlery	Food
Glassware	Wines
Table-cloth	Beers
Napkins	Liqueurs
Salt and pepper	Sherry
Mustard	Spirits
Pickles	Port
Corkscrew	Soft drinks
Swizzle stick	Tea
Can-opener	Coffee
Slices of lemon, orange; cherries etc	Milk and sugar

Picnic menus

Lobster Cocktail with Walnut Bread
Boeuf à la Mode with Four Salads
Strawberry Meringue Baskets

Ham Mousse en Gelée
Dutch Salad
Cheeseboard
Mocha Eclairs

Barbecues

While small barbecues are simple to cater for, large ones can present problems. The main difficulty is timing the food so that all the guests can eat at roughly the same time. Nothing is worse than having guests hanging around for their food and only being able to feed about 10 at a time. There are two solutions to this problem: to hire in sufficient barbecues and barbecue chefs to cook for all the guests simultaneously or to pre-cook the food and simply finish it off on the barbecue.

The first system will depend on the amount of space available and the size of your client's budget. Obviously, hiring extra equipment and extra staff will push the price per head up and you must, of course, have the space to put them. If the client is happy to pay, however, it does mean that the food will be tastier and more authentic than if it is merely finished off over charcoal. The pre-cooking system can be cheaper if the caterer has his own portable cookers which he can bring along. But if he has to hire them, the only saving against the first system will be on staff costs.

Another problem with barbecues in this country is the unreliability of the weather. It is fine if there is room for all the guests to go indoors in the event of rain and the barbecues can be sited under cover, or if the client is prepared to hire a marquee as a fall-back, but if not, the client should be warned that rain—and you don't need a lot of it—could ruin the evening.

Most barbecues are two courses—main and dessert—but sometimes a starter will be required too. Remember that, in addition to the barbecues, tables will be needed to lay out the salads, cheeses, desserts and, of course, the drinks. If the party is a large one you may have to hire in a number of trestle tables. Also remember to allow bigger portions per head as people always seem to have larger appetites when they are eating out of doors.

Wine cups or punches are very popular accompaniments to barbecued food. They can be flamboyant and help make the evening that little bit more special. Do provide alternative drinks though, as some people do not like them. For drink suggestions see Chapter 18.

Barbecue food offers the caterer the opportunity to demonstrate his creative flair with marinades and sauces unless, of course, the client wants plain food. But make sure that your chefs understand fully the techniques of barbecuing, especially for large numbers of people. The food must be cooked at the right height from the coals—if it is too near it will taste of charcoal, and if it is too far away it takes too long to cook. The art of cooking barbecue food well is as demanding as any requirements in the kitchen.

Some barbecuing ideas

Fresh Sardines Served with Lemon Juice
Trout Marinated in Dill and Chive Dressing
and Cooked in Foil
Steaks with Anchovy Butter

Orange Glazed Spare Ribs
Hamburgers with Spicy Sauce
Boned Leg of Lamb with Vinegar and
Thyme Marinade
Duck on a spit with Garlic and Lemon Marinade
Seafood Kebabs with Hollandaise Sauce
Spiced Pork Satay
Lambs' Kidneys on a skewer with Bearnaise Sauce
Bacon Kebabs

Vegetarian food

There are basically two types of vegetarian—lacto-vegetarians and vegans. Lacto-vegetarians cut meat from their diets but are happy to eat milk, cheese and eggs. Vegans eat vegetables, fruit, nuts and grain, eliminating all flesh meat and dairy produce. Some vegans will not eat sugar or honey but will eat soya milk and soya flour cheese. You must therefore find out which sort of vegetarian food your client wants.

Vegetarian food should present no problems for to-day's caterers. There are numerous cookery books which specialise in vegetarian dishes—both lacto and vegan—and probably as many which deal exclusively with vegetable cookery. Eastern food is another good source of ideas for vegetarian dishes and many European dishes such as pizzas, pastas and quiche are either already suitable or can be adapted for vegetarian menus. The less common ingredients for vegetarian dishes are also much easier to buy today as these are usually stocked by health food shops.

Although vegetarian food is not difficult to cook, it is important to experiment so that you become familiar with the tastes, textures and constraints of various dishes. Some vegetarian dishes take a long time to cook as they contain pulses. The following menus will give you some ideas for lacto-vegetarian and vegan menus, quickly prepared food and also a time-consuming menu.

Vegetarian cocktail party
Small Vegetable Samosas
Deep Fried Cauliflower or Aubergine

Banana and Walnut Canapés
Stuffed Artichoke Hearts
Stuffed Mushrooms
Curried Leek Tartlets
Small Onion Bhajias

Vegetarian hot fork buffet
Chick Pea Stroganoff
Vegetarian Chilli
Mushroom and Tomato Pies served with
Caraway Seed Rice and Hot Herb Bread
and Green Salad
Carob and Date Ice Cream

Vegetarian cold fork buffet
Pissaladière
Stuffed Peppers with Spicy Tomato Sauce
Ratatouille Provençale served with Pasta
Salad, Cauliflower in Curried Mayonnaise and
Green Salad
Fresh Fruit Salad
Banana Cream Pie

Chapter 17
Ancillary Services

Catering entails far more than simply supplying food and drink. In many ways it is similar to the entertainment business: presentation must be professional and artistic, service must impress, functions must be stage-managed, timing is crucial, settings and atmospheres must be created and points must be exaggerated for effect. A catering company must, therefore, be prepared to offer its clients all the ancillary services that together complete a successful function.

This may sound a tall order for the one-man business or small firm, but it need entail no more than simply building up a list of reliable suppliers and then hiring their services as and when they are needed. Even the very large catering firms that employ their own full-time flower arrangers and cake decorators will hire in the more specialised ancillary services from time to time.

The small caterer may feel he hasn't the time to spare to organise these extra services but he should remember that the more helpful and varied the service he offers, the better and faster his reputation will grow.

It is important to check the standard of service of all suppliers thoroughly before using them. They must be reliable, professional, efficient and competitively priced. The standard of their service will reflect on you—if it is good, your reputation will profit, if not, your reputation will suffer. Build up a good relationship with the suppliers you use frequently— there will be times when you need to call on them at very short notice and if relations are good, they will be more inclined to pull out all the stops and help out.

If you haven't had to call on a supplier for some

time, make a few enquiries before booking. Changes within the company may have led to a deterioration in the standard of service of which you are quite unaware. And try to have at least two suppliers for each service so that you are not stuck if one is already booked up.

The charge for supplying these extra services can be calculated in two ways. The service can be charged out at the supplier's rate and a consultancy fee added to cover the caterer's costs and profit, or the caterer can add his own percentage to the supplier's fee when invoicing the client. If the cost of the ancillary services amounts to a considerable sum, you may need to ask the client for a deposit in advance.

Though you may start off hiring in all the ancillary services, there will come a time when it makes sense to start supplying some of these in-house. Watch the pattern of demand to see whether there is justification for expanding the business to provide the extra services, bearing in mind that you may be able to hire out the services to other caterers, not just your own clients.

The list of ancillary services is large and varied. Requests can range from something as standard as the supply of marquees to the more unusual, such as the provision of horse-drawn carriages or vintage cars. Country based caterers may find it more difficult than their city colleagues to track down suppliers of the more unusual services, but if the client is prepared to pay, it should be possible to supply almost anything.

Equipment hire

While the larger, more established firms will have their own equipment, new or small companies may have to hire in most of this, which will tend to put them out of the running when competing against large concerns. Rather than incorporate the hire charge in with the menu price, it is a good idea to separate the quote out so that the client can see how the food and hire costs break down. If he is sufficiently impressed with the menus, he may decide to bear the expense of the hire or even to make his own arrangements, such as borrowing equipment from the office canteen.

Most hire firms stock at least two styles of china, one for formal functions and one less formal. There will be choice in plate sizes and shapes too, so the order must stipulate exactly what is required, eg, demi-tasses or full-size coffee cups, soup bowls with or without rims, large or small milk jugs, china or metal condiment sets. Similarly, there will be a choice of cutlery, silver plate or stainless steel. Clear instructions must be given for glasses: are the wine glasses to be hock glasses or Paris goblets, should they be x or y fluid ounces, should beer glasses be straight-sided ones or mugs, half pint or pint? Indicate the sizes of table-cloths as well as the number. Should they be round, square or rectangular?

Tables come in a variety of shapes and sizes, too. You may need to draw up a floor plan to work out the right combination. Allow for the table legs when estimating how many people can be seated and give sufficient space between the tables for waitresses to move to and fro. Should the chairs be the cheaper moulded plastic ones or the more expensive upholstered variety? If posts and rails and coat-racks are required, how many of each will be needed? What heavy equipment will be needed: bains marie, cookers, water-heaters, wine coolers etc? Should these be gas or electric? Most hire firms issue comprehensive brochures, illustrating their stock. If you are familiar with it, then orders can simply be placed over the telephone and followed up with a written order. If hiring for the first time, it will be important to visit the showrooms and see all the articles for yourself. The quality may not be as you had imagined and it may be necessary to find an alternative supplier.

Marquee hire

Hiring a marquee is expensive and the price often comes as a shock to the client. In certain circumstances, however, there may be very strong advantages which outweigh the cost. For example, if a client wants to throw a large party at home but finds his house is too small, a marquee can provide the additional space. If a function is to be held in the open air, a marquee will save the day if there is a downpour. Catering facilities may need to be laid on at a sports ground where there is no pavilion and here again, a marquee would be the answer.

The range of marquees and accessories is very wide and the choice should be discussed in detail with the client well in advance. The number of guests and the ground space will usually dictate the floor space needed. If there is to be a buffet and a disco, two separate tents could be more appropriate than one. When more than one marquee is needed, the shapes and sizes of each will need to be calculated. Should they be totally enclosed or should one of the sides be open? Will awnings and covered walkways be needed? Is it advisable to order floor covering? If so, should this be coconut matting, astro turf, carpeting or wooden boarding? Will it be necessary to lay on power? Does the client want lighting? If so, what form should this take: strip lighting, spot lights, side lighting, chandeliers? If the atmosphere is to be opulent, wall covering and artificial windows and doors can be supplied. Should lavatory tents with portaloos be laid on?

As soon as the choice has been made, the order should be placed. Reputable companies will be booked well in advance and it is important to be able to rely on both the quality of the equipment and the efficiency of the company in delivering and erecting the marquee and then clearing the site afterwards. The hire company may require a deposit and this sum should be added to the general advance paid by the client. When the order is confirmed, make sure the client is informed of the delivery and collection times. Special arrangements may have to be made for someone to be on site to let the vans in. Security passes may have to be issued if the equipment is to be delivered to business premises. Finally, check that delivery and erection are going according to plan on the day—you can't afford to arrive on site with all the food and drink, only to find the marquee has not been delivered.

Cakemaking and decorating

If a company does not employ a skilled baker on its staff, this work can easily be contracted out. There are many people who supply cakes on a freelance basis and most bakers will make and ice cakes to specification.

Choose suppliers who can cope with anything from the traditional wedding cake to novelty cakes calling for imagination and ingenuity. Put together an album with coloured pictures illustrating the range of cakes available. Offer a selection of each type of cake: semi- or fully marzipanned cakes, fruit cakes with or without alcohol, fat-free or flourless cakes, sponge cakes with cream, butter or jam fillings, royal, fondant, butter, frosted or glacé icing. Specify the advance notice needed for the more complicated cakes. Give details of the sizes and weights of the cakes available as well as the number of portions each will serve. Draw up a separate price-list so that this can be updated easily and remember to cost in extras such as boxes, bases and ribbons.

Flower arranging

This work can also be contracted out to either free-lance florists or local businesses. Research into the standard of work of potential suppliers before putting them on your books: do they use only the freshest of flowers, can they work with a variety of materials, do they offer a wide range of displays, do they have a comprehensive stock of vases, bowls, baskets and plinths, how far will they travel, will they work weekends, how competitive are their prices? If possible, talk to people who have used them in the past.

Once you have satisfied yourself on these points, ask for a catalogue and price-list illustrating the range of their work—buttonholes, headdresses, bouquets, sprays, garlands, window boxes and tubs, arrangements with dried or artificial flowers. Many orders will be quite straightforward and simply a matter of the client choosing from the catalogue. Where elaborate and original arrangements are called for, however, the florist should meet the client to discuss things in detail such as themes, colour schemes and the number and sizes of arrangements.

Novelties and printing

Many functions call for novelty gifts or custom printing and you should be able to supply these items when called for. Country based caterers will find they have to search further afield, but suppliers should be found in most cities and large towns. The sort of items that are likely to be in demand are small presents for place settings or lucky dips, crackers, snowballs, masks, streamers, novelty hats, balloons, sparklers and indoor fireworks, printed book matches, printed or novelty napkins, menus, programmes and invitations. Many of the novelties will be cheap, particularly if you are buying in quantity, but custom printing will not, especially if several colours or embossing and cut-outs are involved. Novelties can usually be ordered from suppliers' catalogues, but with printed items, orders will have to be discussed in detail with both the client and the printer. Proofs for all printing work should be cleared by the client in case any last minute alterations need to be made. Most people are not used to dealing with print work, so it is wise to warn the client not to make last minute changes unless absolutely necessary as these are always costly.

Toast-masters

A more accurate name for a toast-master is perhaps a master of ceremonies, for this is the role he plays at formal weddings and dinners. As well as announcing guests as they arrive and calling the toasts, the toast-master tells the speakers exactly what they have to do and when. He then takes charge of events, seeing that each stage of the programme starts and finishes on time and that everything runs according to plan. Most speakers are nervous and a toast-master plays a very important role calming and reassuring everyone. Good toast-masters take a great pride in their

141

work and will have gone through a rigorous training before embarking on their careers. They are experts in the etiquette and ritual of every type of function and will advise and even plan proceedings from beginning to end if the client is unsure of what is required. They should be booked well in advance to avoid disappointment.

Photography

It is impossible to over-emphasise the importance of using only the most reliable and professional photographers. Every function has a very special significance to participants or guests and a photographic record enables people to recall these once in a lifetime moments long after the event is over. Most photographers are reliable and skilled in their work, but there are those who may not turn up on the day or who are such novices that their pictures are as good as useless. Satisfy yourself thoroughly that the photographers on your books are totally reliable and book them early. If video is called for, remember that this involves quite different skills and techniques from still photography. Again, use only firms who specialise in this field and avoid the photographer who dabbles in the work. Make sure that the photographer meets the client before the event for a thorough briefing. If possible they should meet where the function is to be held, as lighting conditions and space may mean that the photographer has to bring along special equipment or that the spot the client has selected for photographs may be unsuitable and a new position needs to be chosen.

Function rooms

Some of the large catering companies have their own reception rooms which they rent out. Smaller firms who are unable to offer this facility may nevertheless be asked to recommend premises from time to time. It is worth compiling a comprehensive list of function rooms throughout your catchment area, calling to see the facilities and meet the people who manage them. If printed details are not available, make a note of the facilities, room dimensions and rentals and update these every year. Making yourself known to the management can be very valuable, as it not only means they will be more inclined to go out of their way to help you, but they may also pass your name on when there are enquiries for caterers.

There are numerous other ancillary services that a caterer may be called upon to provide—singers, bands, discos, comedians, dancers, magicians, Father Christmases, films and videos, coaches, singing telegrams, and so on. In all cases, reliability is the name of the game. Never employ anyone who has not been personally recommended or whose work you are not familiar with. And always make sure they are clearly briefed by either yourself or the client as to exactly what is required of them. In this way you will never disappoint a client and your reputation as a helpful and professional outfit will spread.

Chapter 18
Drink

Large catering concerns and companies at the top end of the market will employ their own specialists whose expertise in the buying, storage, pricing and serving of drink has been built up over a number of years. Employing experts of this calibre will obviously be out of the question for the smaller caterer. His turnover is unlikely to be large enough, and the demand for top quality wines and spirits too small to warrant employing such a specialist.

Nevertheless, the small caterer must be prepared to offer his clients a comprehensive service when supplying drink. It is a very lucrative service to offer because the mark-up on drink in this country is high and, if a caterer does not supply drink, he will lose business to those who do. Drink is an expensive item, one that is subject to deterioration, pilferage, fluctuations in price and quality, and no caterer can afford anything other than the most professional attitude to the buying, storage, selling and service of stocks.

Buying

The four main sources for buying drink are retail outlets, wholesalers, auctions and shippers. Each source has its advantages and disadvantages but in the final analysis it is probably the firm's turnover which decides where to buy.

Retail outlets
Small caterers with a low turnover in drink will probably find they cannot afford to buy in bulk from wholesalers. They might be able to if they form a consortium and share orders with four or five other firms, but this is unlikely to work as their demands

for product, quality and delivery would differ and rarely coincide. Buying wholesale quantities for themselves is likely to be out of the question, as storage would be long term and therefore expensive, wastage might occur if stocks started to deteriorate because they were not being used and, of course, large sums would be tied up in stock when they could be more usefully employed elsewhere.

The most appropriate place to buy drink in these circumstances is the retail shop. Supermarkets and off-licence chains will offer the most competitive prices and the widest selection of well-known brands. Look out for bargain buys and 'own brands' as these are usually excellent value. If you are a regular customer and get to know the people behind the counter, they may even give you advance warning of forthcoming bargain offers which can help you plan some of your buying. Ask their opinion of little known or new lines, as they are often genuinely interested in the business and take a pride in advising customers.

The small specialist off-licence will not normally be able to compete pricewise with the giants but this does not mean to say they should be ruled out altogether. Sometimes they will be the best source of fine wines and spirits. They may specialise in particular lines, and thus for certain functions they would be a more suitable place to shop than the chain stores. Also, the small retailer occasionally offers larger discounts per case than the bigger stores, so the price difference between the two may be less than it seems at first glance. Remember to check discounts and compare the difference from store to store and make enquiries about account facilities. If you are going to be a regular customer the shop should be prepared to offer you an account and this can save you time and money, cutting down the number of cheques you write, and reducing book-keeping entries and paperwork. An account will also give you a month's credit, sometimes more.

Wholesalers
For companies with a faster turnover and a little more storage space, the wholesaler makes the most

suitable source of supply. While prices will not be as cheap as buying direct from the producer, they should be lower than chain store and supermarket prices. Cash and carries can be included here as their prices are usually equivalent to the wholesaler's, but do check this point as sometimes they can be more expensive. Wholesalers don't usually set any minimum purchase rules. Their pricing is generally worked out on a banded basis, for example:

£xxxx)   for 1-5 cases
£xxx) per case for 6-11 cases
£xx   )   for 12-17 cases.

Alternatively, they may offer a discount based on the number of cases bought or it may be up to the client to negotiate what he considers a fair price for the order. Wholesalers will either deliver, which obviously saves the caterer time and money, or goods can be collected after phoning or sending through an order. There are wholesale outlets across the country though, obviously, caterers who are based in rural areas will have less selection and further to travel than town or city based caterers.

Whether the goods are being collected from the cash and carry or wholesaler, or delivered to your premises, remember to check the quantities both at loading and unloading stage. Where drink is concerned it is impossible to be too careful about security because there is so much pilfering.

Auctions

People who buy from auction sales tend to buy in large quantities, or small supplies of extremely fine wines and spirits. Auctions are thus suitable either for the large catering companies or for those dealing with the top end of the market where there is a call for the finest goods.

One of the main advantages of buying at auction is that wines and spirits can be bought at very competitive prices. A disadvantage is that you can never guarantee being successful. The larger auction houses have wine consultants who will be happy to give advice about the various lots being auctioned.

Some have tasting the day before. Inexperienced buyers should be wary of buying without tasting or without advice, as all goods are bought 'as seen' and no auction house will take back a purchase.

There is an art to bidding which, for the inexperienced, can take a little getting used to. The bidding can move at a tremendous speed and the novice may either miss a bid because he is not fast enough or bid above his limit before realising what he has done. It is a good idea to visit a couple of sales just to get used to this before going in to bid yourself. If you are unable to attend on the day you can leave your bids with the auction room staff who will act on your behalf. Different auction houses have different fees which they add to the sale price. Remember to calculate these into your bidding as they can increase the price quite considerably.

While the main auctions are held in London, sales are held all round the country throughout the year.

Shippers
Tremendous savings can be made by buying direct from the producer. The drawback here is that the buyer has to arrange the shipping himself and becomes involved in time-consuming and fiddly paperwork. The solution is to buy direct from the producer, but through a shipping agent. The agent looks after all the shipping arrangements and documents and the buyer simply pays him for this service. The agent's fees are generally reasonable because he has no money at stake in the deal.

Storage

There are two aspects to consider about storage, the economic and the technical.

On the economic side, a caterer must weigh up carefully the price he is paying for the stock against the storage costs from the date of purchase to the day he sells it. Storage is an expensive commodity and unless a firm has its own storage space to spare, it is not usually a viable proposition. Rents for the storage space are likely to cancel out any savings made on

147

bulk purchases or new wines that have to be laid down. And even if the firm has its own storage space, it must consider carefully whether it is sensible to tie up a large amount of its money in stock when it could possibly be used more effectively elsewhere.

On the technical side, the most important factor is to keep the temperature steady — 55°F is a good level to aim at. The worst possible conditions are when the temperature fluctuates, as this puts stresses and strains on the drink. A temperature that is too hot speeds up the maturity rate so will bring stocks on too quickly. Too low a temperature will slow maturity down. Both could cause problems if stock had been laid down for a specific date. Wine must be stored on its side to prevent the corks from drying out. Spirits must be stored upright; if they are laid on their sides the metal caps will eventually rot. Evaporation occurs when the drink is stored in barrels, not once it is sealed in bottles.

Pricing

The formula used by most caterers for pricing wines is fairly straightforward. For quick turnover stock it is normal to double the purchase price and add VAT. If the wines have been laid down for some time, add 10 per cent and compound this each year, then in the year of sale, double the total and add VAT. For example, a case of red wine bought in 1984 for £30 would be sold in 1989 for £90 plus VAT.

For spirits the formula is less rigid and it is best to see what sort of prices the competition is charging.

A mixed bar can be a headache for the small caterer. Larger companies who provide this service on a regular basis can simply count the number of tots consumed and charge the client accordingly. Small companies who are not often called on to provide a mixed bar will probably have to buy in stocks specially for the occasion. They obviously wouldn't want to be left with a whole lot of half full bottles, so the accepted practice here is to charge the client for all the bottles which have been opened and to take back all the unopened bottles. The opened bottles are handed to the client at the end of the function.

Corkage is charged when the client provides the drink himself. In theory, the corkage fee is the normal profit margin a caterer would expect to make on each bottle. In practice this is a bit steep, especially as the caterer has made no financial investment in the drink himself. The best thing to do is to have a look at what the competition charges and fit in with this.

Serving

Serving and presentation is as important with drink as it is with food. Wines must be served at the right temperatures and in the correct glasses. Cocktails must be mixed in the correct proportions and with the right ingredients. Drinks must be presented with the appropriate trimmings: olives, cherries, lemon slices, orange slices and so on. Whether your bar staff are employed on a full- or part-time basis, you must be certain that they are thoroughly trained in serving drink and that they also have a conscientious and professional attitude towards their work.

Be sure, too, that they are honest and, even then, still make strict security arrangements for the drink at all stages: when it is in transit, when it arrives, when it is packed up and when it is returned to the storeroom. Check quantities at each of these stages and when packing up at the end of a function, remember to check the empties as well as the full bottles. One of the oldest tricks in the book is to turn full bottles upside down and place these in a case of empties. Beware, too, of bar staff who are fond of their drink. Sadly, it is one of the hazards of the business that staff often become heavy drinkers or even alcoholics and help themselves to whatever is around. Not only are they then drinking your profits or the client's property, but they may also work less efficiently and even worse, they may get drunk and cause a scene.

Whether you are providing wines, a mixed bar, cocktails or punches, make sure you get an accurate briefing from your client. Some clients will know exactly what they want while others will need guidance. If there is any doubt over the choice of brands, get the client to try samples before finally deciding—it is well worth the trouble and cost to get it right on the day. The sort of points to cover in your briefing are:

Wines

Quality	vin de table
	medium quality
	fine wines

Type	red, white or rosé	French
	sparkling	German
	dry, medium or sweet	Italian
	spritzers	Spanish
		Others

Should a selection be served?
If so, in what proportion?
Should different wines be served with each course
   of the menu?

Mixed bar
selection list:
Sherry—dry, medium, sweet
Port
Madeira
Gin
Whisky
Brandy
Vodka
Rum
Vermouth—red, white, rosé
Wines—red, white, rosé spritzer
       —dry, medium, sweet

Chapter 19
Advertising and Public Relations

Activities aimed at bringing in the business are of paramount importance when you are just starting up. No one has heard of you or used your services and your first job will be to rectify that situation. Even if you have been operating successfully for some time you cannot just sit back and expect the business to continue coming in. Customers can be very fickle. They may decide to try another firm and then stick with them for a while, they may move away or they may just become bored with what you have on offer.

Advertising and public relations activities are aimed at achieving a continuous flow of new business. Depending upon how successful your efforts are you may find that you will need to regulate expenditure in these areas to fit in with seasonal differences in the flow of work or to coincide with the introduction of new services or products. The programme will also need to be dovetailed with plans for direct activity such as mailings and personal visits.

In fact, the main difference between advertising and public relations is that advertising deals with paid-for space in the media ie, newspapers, radio and magazines, whereas public relations is concerned with persuading opinion formers such as newspaper editors, radio presenters, business entertainment organisers and indeed each and every customer to write or talk about your business and its services. Do not underestimate the last item for word-of-mouth recommendation is probably the most important way in which your business becomes known.

Choice of media

To be effective, advertising and public relations

activities must be directed towards the right audience. There is no point, for example, in advertising in *Tatler* magazine if you can only cover a very small area and are specialising in children's parties. Equally, a write-up in the local county magazine will not be very helpful if you want to concentrate on business luncheons.

Take another look at the business proposals which came out of Chapter 1. What kind of services are you planning to offer and who is likely to be interested? The answers to these questions will marry up your plans to the media which these people are likely to take. Children's party givers might well read county magazines or the *Lady*. The businessman, on the other hand, may be more usefully approached through the mail.

Quite often very useful sections of the media get overlooked. Office notice boards, for example, can be a very effective means of local communication, as can theatre programmes or even racing cards. Some media are really only open to paid advertising. Others will be receptive to PR approaches for a simple listing in the shopping column or perhaps for a full-scale interview.

Here's a run down of the kind of media which you should consider, together with an indication of the sort of material they might use. You will have to check for yourself what kind of people receive them and how many.

Television
For most small to medium firms, television advertising is out of the question for it is too expensive. However, the advertisement rates on Channel 4 are nothing like so high as others and may be of interest to larger companies with specialist activities. Each independent television area has separate rates so you need not advertise nationally. TV programme coverage is unlikely but, if you have an outstanding story to tell of rags to riches or the provision of particularly unusual services, they could be interested. Try the editors or producers of the local feature programmes. However, this would be very much a one-off item.

Radio

This is likely to be a much more useful medium for the smaller business. Rates are not very high and most independent local radio stations have facilities for recording simple advertisements. Make sure that the station's catchment area matches your own or you may find yourself travelling rather further than you had planned.

This is also an excellent target area for public relations activities. Most stations—both independent and BBC—are on the look-out for local people to interview. All you need to do is think of an interesting angle. If the interview goes well you might be able to organise a regular spot giving hints and tips on easy entertaining, mixing cocktails or some aspect of specialist cookery. Make sure that you are identified by your business as well as by your own name.

Newspapers

Advertising in national newspapers can be a costly business but it may be a good way to get to your particular target audience. Remember, there are always the personal columns as well as the display ads and these can be much more reasonable. However, if you live outside London and are limited in the distances you are prepared to travel, regional or local newspapers may be a better bet.

Check the circulation areas of the newspapers which serve your catchment area and find out what sort of people read them. Daily papers may have larger circulations than weeklies but they will also be more expensive and have a shorter life. Weekly papers are often kept for the entertainment pages. The best place in the newspaper for your business may be the entertainment pages but it could equally be the business section.

Editorial coverage will be extremely useful in the areas where you are operating. Always send out a press release (see page 156) when you open up and when you offer a new product or service. Some of the jobs you do may also be newsworthy. For example, you may be doing the catering for a big opening or for a VIP visit. If so, ask the people who are organising the publicity for this event to include your business in the write up, and if any reporters attend, give them the details yourself. If you have an uncommon specialty, the local paper may be interested in your story. Approach the person who runs the home page or the shopping column, or failing this, ring the features editor.

Magazines

Both the advertising and the public relations possibilities on magazines are rather similar to those of newspapers. However, magazines have a longer life and they also tend to be aimed more specifically at similar interest groups. In addition to the many national magazines, there are county and local town magazines. These often concentrate on leisure activities and are usually bought by those with a little extra money to spend. House magazines produced for the employees of local firms may also be a useful place to advertise.

Yellow Pages and local directories

The advantage of directory advertising is that it is very local. If you have a business telephone connection you will automatically get a free line entry in your local Yellow Pages. If you are operating from home it is worth making sure that you change over from a private connection. The rental is a little more expensive but the Yellow Pages entry is worth it. An advertisement will, of course, make your entry stand out and the Yellow Pages staff are quite good at helping to draw up a small display ad.

There are also some other reputable local directories but, if you are approached by a local directory salesman, make sure his directory really does exist for there are spurious ones around. There are also some organisations which specialise in solving people's problems and it could be a good investment to get on to their lists too.

Programmes

If you have a local theatre, a special sports stadium or race course, it could be worth advertising in these.

Theatre-goers may well be heavy entertainers and race-goers could be in the market for special packed lunches. County shows, horse trials and motor racing offer other opportunities. The decision to advertise should depend upon your assessment of how many of the people at the particular event in question are likely to be interested in your kind of services.

Notice boards
These can be a very useful form of communication and often a very reasonable one. If your business is small scale and local in its operations, use shop window boards where it will not be difficult to make your card stand out. Simply type it neatly or, better still, letraset it. Club and office notice boards can be equally effective at bringing in business. Approach the club secretary for the former and the personnel manager for the latter. Keep your card small and neat—it should not take up too much space on the board.

Direct mail
With direct mail your message goes straight to the home of the private client or to the desk of the business client. Compiling a list of suitable addresses may take a little time but the local Yellow Pages, engagement announcements in the local papers and street directories can all help. You could also have your message hand delivered to houses in areas which your market research indicates to be filled with potential customers. Write a covering letter setting out details of your services and enclose any suitable promotional literature.

The tools

To be really effective in the advertising and public relations field it is not enough to choose the right media outlets, you must also get your message across. This means that you will need to give some careful thought to the content and design of your advertisements and direct mail shots and to the content of any press release.

The secret is not to try to be too clever. Stick to the point in all your promotional material and simply set out the details of the services you have to offer with reference to the way in which they can make life easier and pleasanter for the recipients.

Advertisements
The telephone sales people on newspaper and Yellow Pages advertising desks are often trained to help in putting together simple advertisements. Nevertheless, it is sensible to have some idea of what you want to do. Take a look at competitive advertisements and see which ones strike you as being the most effective. Good clear lettering stands out better than script or italics and this, coupled with a simple drawing, may be the answer. Make sure that the name of your business is easy to read and that the entry includes your telephone number and address. A simple line such as, 'Let us arrange your Party for all Special Occasions' could sum up your business very well. However, if you do have any special services to offer such as vegetarian cuisine, special theme cakes or barbecues, put that in too, but take care not to overcrowd the advertisement. Take a larger space if you have a lot to say.

Direct mail letters
Once again the key is brevity. The recipient does not want to read long eulogies about your own company. All he might want to know are what services you have to offer. You can always extol their virtues in greater detail if you get an enquiry.

The contents of such letters must, of course, relate to the recipient so that a letter to potential business customers will be rather different from a letter to a club secretary.

Press releases
These are really quite easy to write. Stick to the facts and resist the temptation to pad things out. Get as much information as you can into the first few sentences or paragraph and develop the more interesting points in subsequent paragraphs. This makes it much easier for an editor to cut to a particular length

or to lift out sections to fit in with a shopping column or services round-up.

Send out a release when you open up and whenever you have new services to offer or when you have fulfilled a particularly interesting or unusual job. Send a photograph, if possible, with the latter. Remember to add the contact details at the base of every release sent out and fix the release firmly to the picture.

Here's an example of a starting-up release. Sample menus should be included with such a release.

NEW CATERING SERVICE FOR SUSSEX
Barbecues, Picnics & Outdoor Food a Speciality
A new catering service specialising in outdoor food of all kinds is now on offer from Teddy Bears' Picnics of 6 Alton Road, Farmbridge, Sussex. Phone 0000 11111. Orders can be delivered any time, anywhere within the county boundaries.

The barbecue service includes preparation on or off site, delivery of the food and clearing away. Service, equipment hire, special theme/support and drinks can also be arranged.

Picnics and special hampers for Glyndebourne and other artistic and sporting events in Sussex are another speciality of the new service. Prices range from £3 per head for simple picnic baskets to £10 plus for special events hampers.

Teddy Bears' Picnics also offer indoor party catering, specialising in theme birthdays and anniversaries and children's parties.

For further information contact:
A Anon, Proprietor
Teddy Bears' Picnics
6 Alton Road,
Farmbridge, Sussex
Tel: 0000 11111

Chapter 20
Dealing with Clients

Your day-to-day dealings with customers and clients can be equally important in keeping the business flowing in. Indeed, in some ways this is just as much a part of your public relations programme as sending out press releases or talking on the radio. A happy and satisfied client is one who is likely to come back to you, but a disgruntled one will not and he may even put other potential customers off.

Dealing with people is not always easy and it can take much patience and tact to handle someone who seems determined to be difficult. Keep the old adage that the customer is always right to the forefront of your mind—even when he is not! No one will thank you for showing him up or proving him wrong, so tread carefully even when you know you are in the right.

A firm and friendly approach is equally important and you must appear to know what you are doing. After all, a customer needs to believe that you are an expert in your field and will not let him down on what to him might be an extremely important occasion. In short, you should try to project an image of competence and reliability, and the best way of doing this is to *be* competent and reliable. Don't make promises you cannot fulfil and avoid the temptation to take on business when really you are fully stretched.

Starting the dialogue

The first step is to have an efficient and helpful answering system for enquiries. If you are a small one-man band this may mean a really friendly and welcoming message on the answerphone machine. This is very important as there are lots of people who do not like speaking to a machine and feel intimidated by an abrupt instruction to talk after the bleep.

Some small firms opt for a personal answering service. This may be on a separate number or linked to one or more of your own numbers. Larger firms may have receptionist/telephonists who take the calls initially and can be trained to deal with customer enquiries in the absence of more senior management. In both these circumstances it is a good idea to ring up yourself to see what sort of greeting and response are given, and ask some friends to ring in with fictional enquiries and to make notes on how they are dealt with.

Once contact is made between the potential customers and the person who will be organising the event, the emphasis must be on eliciting as much information as possible. It is important both for the customer and for your planning to get all the facts at the start.

Some customers are not really sure exactly what they want and the initial conversation should be aimed at helping the client to make up his mind without pushing him into something that he might regret afterwards. Other customers seem to know exactly what they want and though this may be a help, it can also have its drawbacks. The potential client's ideas may not be practicable, they may be cutting the corners on staff and they could be contrary to the knowledge which you have of what makes a successful event. If this is the case you will have to use a good deal of tact to change the customer's ideas without antagonising him.

The dialogue with the customer should continue during the planning stages for an event through to the day itself. You ignore your customer at your peril. Communication at crucial stages ensures that you are all thinking along the same lines and helps to eliminate the possibility of misunderstandings. It also reduces anxiety on the part of the client which makes life easier for all concerned.

It should go without saying that you must listen to your client but some caterers are surprised that, at the end of the day, their client is not happy with the arrangements even though there was consultation at every stage. Of course, there are occasions when it seems that customers are being unreasonable, but check your own notes before blaming them.

Problem customers

There should not really be any of these if you are doing your job well but some people can be difficult, sometimes, it seems, just for the sake of it! Every client is a law unto him or herself but here are a few typical problem customers with some tips on how to deal with them.

The vacillating customer can drive you round the bend with continual phone calls changing some aspect of the plans for his event. First he will change the menu, then the time the food is to be served, then the drinks and then the menu again. He will order flowers and cancel them and then blame you if there are no floral decorations on the day. The only way to deal with this kind of customer is to be as firm as possible and to try to discourage too many changes. Confirm in writing the changes he does insist on so you cannot be blamed for them later.

Most customers tend to worry about their event, but they worry particularly about the time you are to arrive and about the quantity of food. Regarding the time of arrival, do keep to what was agreed in the first instance, or if you decide that you do not need to arrive so early, ring up and let your customer know. You will get off to a bad psychological start if the customer is in a panic over your non-arrival. With regard to the quantities, things can be the other way round so don't let your customer panic *you*!

You may have some customers who do not know how to treat staff. Of course, you will not know this the first time you cater for them but on a subsequent occasion you can alert your waiting staff and assistant cooks to the fact that the client may be rather offhand or that he is particularly exacting or difficult. Forewarned is usually forearmed and you do not want your staff leaving you because of the actions of one client.

Dissatisfied customers, on the other hand, should be listened to with some care. Encourage customers to make their complaints direct to you, but do also make sure that your staff come to you with any complaints from customers, then check things out in detail. Once you have the facts you will be in a much better position to deal with the complaint. Direct apologies may be needed; if so do give them personally and in writing, possibly with some offer to make amends. Even if you do not think that your operation is at fault, it is worth listening carefully to complaints for they could arise from misunderstandings or simply from bad communication. You may find quite simple remedies to ensure that the same thing does not happen again.

Customers who are late in paying or who do not pay at all are the worst of the problem customers. You must first make sure that each customer has been informed of and understands the terms of payment. The next step is to send out reminders promptly. Do not let things slide; everyone tends to pay those who press for payment sooner rather than those who do not follow up very quickly.

If you still do not get paid you may have to send a solicitor's letter or even resort to the courts, which does not have to be too costly. There are various procedures which you can put into action without any specialist legal advice and these are worth finding out about. Talk to the Small Firms Centres and go to the local law centre. Some private firms even run courses on efficient debt collecting.

Follow through

Good after-sales service in terms of clearing away, collection of hired equipment, the despatch of wedding cake and the like all help to create a good impression with customers. It is also worth checking to see if there are any other events linked to the main one which might require catering.

A general follow-up letter after the job has been completed is a good idea and this might be followed up with six-monthly or yearly contact to see if any other major events are to be planned: every client is a potential customer for your mailing lists. Clients who have arranged Christmas parties with you should be contacted in good time for the following year's event, wedding breakfast clients could become dinner party or buffet party customers and children's party customers may be interested in summer picnics or barbecues.

A Christmas card featuring one of your latest menus is another way of keeping in touch and you will probably be able to think of some more creative ideas.

Chapter 21
Presentation

Good presentation is always important when dealing with food. Nobody wants to eat food, however wholesome, which looks boring. On the other hand, an attractively presented buffet can turn relatively inexpensive food into a delight.

Cocktail snacks

With cocktail snacks good presentation is absolutely vital. Your pâté canapés may taste out of this world, but they will need finishing off with some decoration or garnish before they even begin to look appetising. It is therefore worth spending some time considering how to decorate each item and then picture the different combinations laid out on a tray.

Even the humblest food can look attractive: coat quarters of Scotch egg with a layer of aspic, sprinkle cocktail sausages liberally with mixed herbs, decorate sausage rolls with pastry leaves and flowers, cut sandwiches into different shapes—hearts, half moons, diamonds, etc. Once you start to give some thought to this aspect, you will be surprised to find how easy it is to come up with some quite original ideas.

Laying up the trays needs careful thought too. A tray of nothing but vol au vents will lack colour, life and interest. Mix five or six different foods on a tray and arrange them in patterns such as diagonals or circles. A centre-piece on a tray will also look most attractive. Place a cushion of watercress in the middle of the tray and stud this with flower heads. Cover half a potato with holly leaves and berries and dust this with silver frosting. Fill a small bowl with crushed ice, lay prawns in their shells and lemon slices on top and then sprinkle it with freshly chopped parsley. For dramatic effects you can really go to town using lighted sparklers and candles to decorate the food.

Whether you are providing simple or exotic food, remember to tidy the trays each time they come back to the kitchen for replenishing. The centre-pieces will need freshening up and the doilies get greasy very quickly so will need changing frequently. Some waitresses just can't be bothered to stop and tidy the trays up, so it is worth assigning someone reliable to check each one before it goes out.

Finger buffets

Presentation will generally be less fancy than for cocktail food but, on the other hand, it can be more difficult to make it look attractive. Things like chicken drumsticks and slices of quiche can look pretty dull and stodgy. Bring the trays to life with colourful garnishes: slices of orange with watercress, tomatoes and shredded lettuce, grated carrots with green and red peppers and black olives. Use swags of greenery or attractive centre-pieces to decorate the table and link these to the theme of the function or to the season.

Simple flower arrangements aren't too difficult to put together provided you are not too ambitious with the size and shape. If the client is willing to pay, employ a professional florist to take care of this. A mountain of fresh fruit featuring some unusual tropical fruits can make a very attractive display which does not demand great artistic talent on your part. For more exotic displays, make an arrangement of shell fish on ice and decorate this with flowers and greenery, or make a display of game birds with their colourful plumage.

Fork buffets

The imaginative displays described above will also look good on a fork buffet table. Here the emphasis will be on larger quantities of a small number of dishes.

Cold food is relatively easy to decorate. Hams, cold turkeys and chicken can be decorated in a chaud-froid sauce or in aspic. Make up designs with bay leaves, black peppercorns, sliced stuffed olives and the like.

Salad materials such as radishes, spring onions and tomatoes can all be cut into flower shapes, and watercress, parsley—particularly the continental variety—and salad leaves can be used to give a splash of contrasting green. Hot foods can be garnished with pastry fleurons and fried bread triangles as well as the inevitable lemon wedge and watercress.

Sit-down meals

Presentation here becomes more a matter of excellence and service. Dishes should look good as they are brought to the table but inevitably they start to lose some of their extreme attractiveness as they are served. Table centre-pieces, which should not be too high, and good glassware and cutlery help to set the scene. Shaded colour combinations of table linen, perhaps to match the decor of the room, personalised menus as well as written place names, can also enhance the table.

Finally, do remember that, important though good presentation can be, it will not make up for bad quality food or inadequate service. In the end it is a consistently high standard of food and service which will bring the business back.

Appendix

Catering and cookery courses

- ● Offers short courses: weekends, full week, single day or one day for a number of consecutive weeks.
- ★ Offers a three-month or longer diploma course.
- ○ Offers two- to four-week courses.

● **Blackdown Hall**
Haslemere, Surrey

★ **Bouquet Garni School of Cookery**
117 Dorset Road, London SW19

● **Catercall Cookery Courses**
5 Lawn Road, London NW3 2XS

● **Claudia Roden's Middle Eastern Cookery**
8 Wild Hatch, London NW11

● **Cooks Workshop**
4 Cadogan Mansions, Sloane Square,
London SW1

● ★ **Cordon Bleu Cookery School (London) Ltd**
114 Marylebone Lane, London W1M 6HH

● **CuisinEase**
56 Holland Park Road, London W14

● **Divertimenti Cookery School**
139-41 Fulham Road, London SW3

● **The Earnly Concourse**
Earnly, Nr Chichester, Sussex PO20 7JL

★ **Ewert Place School of Cookery**
1 Ewert Place, Summertown,
Oxford OX2 7XD

● **Farthinghoe Fine Wine and Food**
The Old Rectory, Farthinghoe,
Brackley, Northants

● ○ **The Grange**
Beckington, Nr Bath, Avon BA3 6TD

- **Green Apple**
  Church Corner, Youlgreave, Bakewell,
  Derbyshire DE4 1WL
- ★ **The Jane Mann School of Cookery**
  10 Tyrawley Road, London SW6 4QQ
- **John Tovey's Four Day Pastry Course**
  Miller Howe, Windermere, Cumbria LA23 1EY
- **Ken Lo's Kitchen**
  14 Eccleston Street, London SW1
- ★ ○ **L'Academie de la Cuisine et du Vin**
  50 Hill Rise, Richmond, Surrey TW10 6UB
- ★ **Leith's School of Food and Wine**
  21 St Alban's Grove, London W8 5BP
- **Let's Cook with Suzy**
  Suzy Benghiat, 156a Old Brompton Road,
  London SW5 0BE
- ★ **Malvern School of Cookery**
  9 Guarlford Road, Malvern WR14 3OW
- **Master Classes in Food and Wine**
  27 Gibwood Road, Northenden,
  Manchester M22 4BR
- **The Microwave Cooking School**
  Apple Tree Cottage, 2b South Hill Park,
  London NW3
- ★ **Mrs Elizabeth Pomeroy School of Cookery**
  51 Hornton Street, London W8 7NT
- ★ **Mrs Elizabeth Russell**
  18 The Grange, London SW19 4PS
- **Mrs Laurence's Cookery Courses**
  The Grooms, East Lydford,
  Somerton, Somerset
- **Mrs Sonia Stevenson's Weekend Courses
  for Sauces**
  The Horn of Plenty Restaurant, Culworthy,
  Tavistock, Devon
- **Rookery Hall (Cookery Enjoyment Courses)**
  Worleston, Nr Nantwich, Cheshire CW5 6DQ
- ★ **Sabine de Mirbeck Ecole de Cuisine Francaise**
  Clapham House, Litlington,
  Sussex BN26 5RQ
- **Sue Probert—Cooking at Home**
  35 Cliffe Hill, Coventry Road,
  Warwick CV34 5HN

★ **Tante Marie School of Cookery**
Woodham House, Carlton Road, Woking,
Surrey GU21 4HF
● **The Vegetarian Society**
53 Marloes Road, London W8 6LA
● ★ **Winkfield Place**
Winkfield, Windsor, Berkshire SL4 4RN

Useful addresses

National telephone dialling codes are given, though
local codes may differ.

Local councils, tourist boards and Chambers of
Commerce can be good sources of help and information. Many organisations listed below will have local
offices.

**Advisory, Conciliation and Arbitration Service
(ACAS)**
Head Office, 11-12 St James's Square,
London SW1Y 4LA; 01-214 6000

Alliance of Small Firms and Self-Employed People
42 Vine Road, East Molesey, Surrey KT8 9LF;
01-979 2293

British Hotels, Restaurants and Caterers Association
40 Duke Street, London W1M 6HR; 01-499 6641

**Council for Small Industries in Rural Areas
(CoSIRA)**
141 Castle Street, Salisbury, Wiltshire SP1 3TP;
0722 336255

**Department of Employment,
Small Firms Division**
Freefone Enterprise for all regional offices.

Food and Drink Industries Council
25 Victoria Street, London SW1H 0BX;
01-222 1533

Health and Safety Commission
Regina House, 259 Old Marylebone Road,
London NW1 5RR; 01-723 1262

Health and Safety Executive
25 Chapel Street, London NW1 5DT; 01-262 3277

HM Customs and Excise
VAT Administration Directorate,
King's Beam House, Mark Lane,
London EC3R 7HE; 01-283 8911

HM Stationery Office
PO Box 276, London SW8; 01-211 8815
(enquiries)

Industrial and Commercial Finance Corporation
91 Waterloo Road, London SE1 8XP;
01-928 7822

Registrar of Companies
Companies House, Crown Way, Maindy,
Cardiff CF4 3UZ; 0222 388588

102 George Street, Edinburgh EH2 3DJ;
031-225 5774

43-7 Chichester Street, Belfast BT1 4RJ;
0232 234121

Further reading

Consumer Law for the Small Business,
    Patricia Clayton (Kogan Page)
The Cookery Year (Reader's Digest)
Cooking by the Dozen, Elizabeth Pomeroy
    (Hamlyn)
*Croner's Reference Book for the Self-employed and
    Smaller Business* (Croner Publications)
*Financial Management for the Small Business,
    The Daily Telegraph Guide*, Colin Barrow
    (Kogan Page)
*Law for the Small Business, The Daily Telegraph
    Guide*, 4th edn, Patricia Clayton (Kogan Page)
Mastering the Art of French Cooking,
    Simone Bech, Louiselle Berthole and Julia Childs
    (Penguin Books)
The Modern Patissier, William Barber (Northwood)
    Publications)
New Larousse Gastronomique (Hamlyn)

Sunday Telegraph Good Wine Guide, published
   annually
Which? Wine Guide, published annually by the
   Consumers' Association (Hodder & Stoughton)
*Working for Yourself: the Daily Telegraph Guide
   to Self-Employment*, 8th edn, Godfrey Golzen
   (Kogan Page)

Journals
Caterer and Hotelkeeper, Quadrant House,
   The Quadrant, Sutton, Surrey SM2 5AS
Catering, 161-5 Greenwich House,
   Greenwich High Street, London SE10 8JA
Catering and Hotel Management, Link House,
   Dingwall Avenue, Croydon, Surrey CR9 2AT
Catering Times, Quadrant House, The Quadrant,
   Sutton, Surrey SM2 5AS
Decanter, 16 Blackfriars Lane, London EC4V 6EB
Gourmet Magazine (US publication; can be ordered
   through newsagents)
Vogue, Vogue House, Hanover Square, London W1
Which? Wine Monthly, Consumers' Association,
   14 Buckingham Street, London WC2N 6DS

Index